Stereotyping Religion II

CRITIQUING RELIGION: DISCOURSE, CULTURE, POWER

Series editor: Craig Martin

Critiquing Religion: Discourse, Culture, Power publishes works that historicize both religions and modern discourses on "religion" that treat it as a unique object of study. Using diverse methodologies and social theories, volumes in this series view religions and discourses on religion as commonplace rhetorics, authenticity narratives, or legitimating myths, which function in the creation, maintenance, and contestation of social formations. Works in the series are on the cutting edge of critical scholarship, regarding "religion" as just another cultural tool used to gerrymander social space and distribute power relations in the modern world. *Critiquing Religion: Discourse, Culture, Power* provides a unique home for reflexive, critical work in the field of religious studies.

Christian Tourist Attractions, Mythmaking and Identity Formation
Edited by Erin Roberts and Jennifer Eyl

French Populism and Discourses on Secularism
Per-Erik Nilsson

Reframing the Masters of Suspicion: Marx, Nietzsche, and Freud
Andrew Dole

Religion, Nationalism and Foreign Policy
Filiz Coban Oran

Representing Religion in Film
Edited by Tenzan Eaghll and Rebekka King

Rethinking Christian Martyrdom: The Blood is the Seed?
Matt Recla

Spirituality, Corporate Culture, and American Business: The Neoliberal Ethic and the Spirit of Global Capital
James Dennis LoRusso

Stereotyping Religion: Critiquing Clichés
Edited by Brad Stoddard and Craig Martin

Stereotyping Religion II

Critiquing Clichés

**EDITED BY
BRAD STODDARD AND
CRAIG MARTIN**

BLOOMSBURY ACADEMIC
LONDON • NEW YORK • OXFORD • NEW DELHI • SYDNEY

BLOOMSBURY ACADEMIC
Bloomsbury Publishing Plc
50 Bedford Square, London, WC1B 3DP, UK
1385 Broadway, New York, NY 10018, USA
29 Earlsfort Terrace, Dublin 2, Ireland

BLOOMSBURY, BLOOMSBURY ACADEMIC and the Diana logo are
trademarks of Bloomsbury Publishing Plc

First published in Great Britain 2023

Copyright © Craig Martin, Brad Stoddard and contributors, 2023

Craig Martin and Brad Stoddard have asserted their rights under the Copyright,
Designs and Patents Act, 1988, to be identified as Editors of this work.

For legal purposes the Acknowledgments on p. ix constitute an extension
of this copyright page.

Series design by Dani Leigh
Cover image © Yi Lu / EyeEm. Getty Images

Bloomsbury Publishing Plc does not have any control over, or responsibility for, any
third-party websites referred to or in this book. All internet addresses given in this
book were correct at the time of going to press. The author and publisher regret any
inconvenience caused if addresses have changed or sites have ceased to exist,
but can accept no responsibility for any such changes.

A catalogue record for this book is available from the British Library.

A catalogue record for this book is available from the Library of Congress.

ISBN: HB: 978-1-3502-6358-1
PB: 978-1-3502-6359-8
ePDF: 978-1-3502-6360-4
eBook: 978-1-3502-6361-1

Series: Critiquing Religion: Discourse, Culture, Power

Typeset by Deanta Global Publishing Services, Chennai, India

To find out more about our authors and books visit www.bloomsbury.com and
sign up for our newsletters

We dedicate this to our students

Contents

Acknowledgments

Brad Stoddard and Craig Martin would like to thank our many students, who helped bring to our attention those stereotypes or clichés that we missed in our first volume. We would also like to thank everyone who contributed to this volume and the team at Bloomsbury, especially Lalle Pursglove and Lily McMahon. It's always a pleasure to work with you.

Introduction

A few years ago (when news about the Islamic State in Syria was making international headlines), Craig was visiting extended family. After a family reunion event, a group of folks went over to the home of one of the de facto matriarchs of the family, a woman in her late sixties or early seventies. After having served her company drinks and snacks, she sat down to chat with everyone. At one point, the conversation took a sharp turn, as she turned toward Craig and asked something like the following: "Craig, you teach religion, right? Maybe you can answer this: Why do Muslims want to kill everyone and cut their heads off?"

Craig was taken aback, but retorted with his own question: "What makes you think all Muslims want to kill people?" She and her husband responded nonverbally, as they both pointed at the television at the center of the room.

Long-standing research in social psychology demonstrates that it is difficult to upset people's stereotypes, as humans appear to suffer from confirmation bias—the tendency to pay attention to things that confirm our stereotypes and ignore things that contradict our stereotypes. You can produce mountains of counterevidence to someone's stereotypes, but it may not matter as long as they have even a little evidence—no matter how slim—that confirms the stereotype. It did not help, in this circumstance, that the question made Craig angry, which prompted an angry response; it is hard to take serious evidence that contradicts our stereotypes, and even harder when that evidence comes from a hostile source. In any case, Craig attempted to make the case that (1) most Muslims do not have homicidal tendencies and (2) there are people who advocate for or participate in violence in all religious traditions (there are, in fact, even militant Buddhists, despite the common image of the peaceful Buddhist monk). At the end of the day, she and her husband were unpersuaded; the only Muslims they knew about were the murderous ones they heard about daily on the television, and they sure as hell weren't going to take seriously the ramblings of an angry young nephew who appeared to be biased.

For Craig, a scholar of religion who in fact has personally known many Muslims and who has several Muslim friends, evidence contrary to her stereotype was easy to come by: he's had brilliant Muslim students, kind Muslim mentors, friendly Muslim drinking buddies, and so on. Craig has met many Muslims, but he's never met one with homicidal tendencies. However, in north, rural Indiana, such experiences with Muslims are harder to come by. It's no wonder why this older relative might have doubted him. As a result, it is also no surprise that she politically supported the US wars against predominantly Muslim countries in the last two decades or that she proudly voted for a president who, upon taking office, immediately put in place a "Muslim ban" designed to limit entry into the US for people from the Middle East. *The stereotypes we hold shape the politics we support. Stereotypes have social and political consequences.*

*   *   *

To identify and challenge some of the more pervasive and problematic clichés about religion, in 2017, we edited and published a volume titled *Stereotyping Religion: Critiquing Clichés*. That volume attempted to identify ten of the more common clichés about religion; it summarized the clichés' histories, and it identified potential problems with these clichés. The book considered clichés such as "religions are belief systems," "religions are intrinsically violent," "religion makes people moral," and "learning about religion leads to tolerance." We hoped that it would help our students and other undergraduates reconsider common clichés about religion. While teaching the volume in classes, however, we encountered an unexpected problem. Our students, most of whom were two decades younger than us, hadn't heard of some (or, in some instances, most) of the clichés! Instead of problematizing long-held clichés, these students simultaneously learned that the clichés exist as they learned to question them. In other words, the students learned about the clichés only for the sake of dismissing them.

Conversations in classrooms progressed as we asked our students to identify some of the claims about religion they frequently encountered in their lives. Not surprisingly, they reported claims that addressed issues that were relevant to their most immediate political and sociocultural interests. Specifically, claims related to sexuality, abortion, birth control, and other so-called culture war issues emerged as common themes. Why can't religious people separate their religion from politics? Why are all religions against LGBTQIA+ rights? Why can't all religions embrace religious pluralism? And why do religion and science have to conflict? These are a few of the more common ideas they expressed in class.

Having learned about clichés in *Stereotyping Religion: Critiquing Clichés*, however, we asked our students if these, too, can be clichés. Do these ideas similarly have their own histories? Their own advocates? Their own political implications? The answer was obviously yes. To address these clichés and to provide a book more suited to a younger audience, we began the work that resulted in the publication of this book.

As this suggests, this volume was literally born in the classroom and addresses many of the clichés that our students encounter, provided those students are in the United States and are in the age group generally classified as Gen Z. As a result, this volume will speak to them, their interests, and their cultures more than the previous volume. The potential problem, however, is that the current volume is more focused on the United States and not as relevant to audiences outside the United States. To mitigate this potential problem, the editors and the authors agreed that many of the issues addressed in this volume have parallels outside the United States and that these transnational issues often share common histories. So, while the chapters in this volume are more focused on the United States, we highlight transnational and transhistorical parallels when possible and applicable.

Following the format established in the previous volume, this volume tackles ten stereotypes about religion. In the chapters that follow, Savannah H. Finver, Rita Lester, and Jacob Barrett problematize clichés about religious freedom and the relationship between religion and government. Leslie Dorrough Smith and James Crossley address clichés related to conservative religious traditions and their treatment of gender and sexuality. We (i.e., Brad Stoddard and Craig Martin) and Ting Guo explore common assumptions about spirituality, its relation to religion, and its connection with Asian or "Eastern" religions. David Robertson argues that while members of a particular religion tend to believe that there is an authentic and unchanging core uniting all the religion's members over time and space, religions change significantly over time as people embrace different ideas and respond to constantly changing political, economic, and sociocultural environments. Donovan Schaefer questions the alleged incompatibility of religion and science or the assumption that they are somehow opposites. Martha Smith Roberts demonstrates that although religious pluralism presents itself as infinitely open-minded and tolerant, pluralism is, in practice, always closed toward someone.

* * *

In order to help contextualize the chapters that follow, we would like to point to some common themes or scholarly assumptions the authors make.

Some of the following chapters discuss what scholars refer to as "orientalism." As we summarize in our chapter on spirituality, the concept of orientalism was first explored by Edward Said in his book *Orientalism*. There Said argued that European literature and history throughout the modern period were saturated with a systematic set of assumptions about fundamental differences between "the orient"—that is, "the East"—and "the occident"—that is, "the West." Those in Europe developed stereotypes about themselves by imagining themselves as superior to those in other parts of the world: "European identity [was] a superior one in comparison with all the non-European peoples and cultures" (Said 1978, 7). Orientalism assumed that the West was rational, dynamic and changing, and more civilized, while the

East—especially Islam—was less rational and perhaps more mystical, stuck in the past, static and unchanging, and lacked civilization. The Islamophobic stereotypes contained in orientalism permitted Europeans to feel superior to and look down upon Arabs, who were considered socially and civilizationally backward; for Said, those stereotypes contributed to legitimating European colonization of the Muslim Arab world.

Orientalism—like all cultural traditions—has evolved over time. The forms of orientalism that contrasted "the West" with the Arab world are in some ways considerably different from those that contrast "the West" with Asian and South Asian religious traditions. The forms of orientalism that contrast, for instance, Hinduism and Buddhism with Judaism, Christianity, and Islam often romanticize rather than demonize Hinduism and Buddhism. To some extent the stereotypes are similar: "the East" is thought to be more mystical, stuck in the past, and static and unchanging—but these are inflected with positive rather than negative associations. American cinema repeatedly uses this cliché: in so many US films, "Westerners" have traveled to "Shangri-La" or the "mystic East" in order to discover truths that Western cultures have apparently lost or forgotten. Such travelers find themselves climbing steps to a temple high on a mountain, where monks reside who keep alive traditions that are thousands of years old—which they can apparently do because they are seemingly stuck in the past, static and unchanging, and unaffected by Western culture or civilization. Recent films or television shows that utilize such stereotypes include *Bulletproof Monk* (2003), *The Last Samurai* (2003), *Kill Bill 2* (2004), *Batman Begins* (2005), *Kung Fu Panda* (2008), *The Forbidden Kingdom* (2008), *Doctor Strange* (2016), and *Iron Fist* (2017–18). While the stereotype that Asians have access to ancient, mystical truths lost to folks in "the West" is more positive than the stereotype that Muslims are backward savages, *it is still a stereotype*, and one that glosses over the fact that Asian nations change just as much as European ones. As Ting Guo notes in her chapter, this cliché underestimates the "modern sociopolitical transformations of those societies and the changing manifestations of religions in those places." Tibetan monasteries change as much with the times as do American Christians.

Though this might be surprising to many students who think they're "only" reading a book about religion, the issue of taxonomy weighs heavily in this volume and spans multiple chapters. Taxonomy, of course, refers to classification—that is, to the ways we organize and classify things into the categories we've inherited through the socialization process that teaches us about dominant and local cultures and about our place in said cultures. As sociologists have repeatedly demonstrated, societies function when they present arbitrary classifications as self-evident and obvious. To understand this point, consider the taxonomic distinction between cow shit and manure.

It's probably safe to assume that most of us were taught to avoid cow shit. More likely, most of us rarely, if ever, interact with cow shit, but in the socialization process, we probably learned that if we do encounter cow shit, we should avoid it. We definitely shouldn't purchase it, bring it into our yards, bury our hands in it for the sake of relaxing or unwinding after a hard day's work, and pluck food out of it that we subsequently eat. While most of us probably cringe at the thought of digging our hands deep into cow shit, that's precisely what people do when they use manure.

People in the United States routinely purchase cow shit—that is, manure—and they mix it with dirt (usually called soil—another taxonomic sleight of hand to disguise what's happening) for the sake of enhancing one's plants and vegetables. We know of no one who looks forward to playing with cow shit and dirt, but day after day, people across the nation do precisely that when they mix manure with soil. That is, gardeners and farmers take the same substance and develop multiple terms (i.e., classifications) to designate how and when it's acceptable to avoid the substance or to interact with it. Returning to the previous point about taxonomy and making the arbitrary seem natural, there is no inherent distinction between cow shit and manure, yet very few people question this distinction because we are socialized into a culture that embraces this distinction. We internalize this distinction and rarely think twice about the significance of burying our hands in cow shit and of eating food that grows in it. In short, we learn to distinguish cow shit from manure, and we adjust our behaviors and expectations based on this arbitrary distinction. What does any of this have to do with religion or about clichés related to religion?

Many of the clichés about religion are similarly based on arbitrary taxonomic distinctions that exist in our culture, that haven't always existed in the United States, and that don't exist in other cultures and other parts of the world. For example, is a belief a religious belief, a political belief, or maybe even a spiritual belief? Is an action motivated by religion or by culture? These nouns (religion, spirituality, culture, and politics) may seem self-evident to us because we are born into a cultural system that uses these terms. We might disagree (and we do!) over definitions of terms like religion and spirituality, but our shared assumption that they are taxonomic "things"—that is, that they exist—allow them to function in our society. Several of the chapters in this volume question this basic assumption. They identify seemingly arbitrary distinctions and they question the clichés that we build on top of them.

One thing to keep in mind when thinking about classification is that some terms are politically useful because of their positive and negative associations. Some distinctions carry few, if any, moral or ethical associations. Presumably no one goes to battle over the distinction between "green" and "olive green"—whether we classify my backpack as "green" or "olive" green likely has no social or political consequences. However, many of the distinctions or terms discussed in this volume are *normative*, meaning that they imply value judgments about whatever falls under the terms. A classic example is the distinction between "terrorist" and "freedom fighter"; most individuals classified as terrorists likely understand themselves not as terrorists but rather as those fighting for the freedom of their homeland. Whether we call someone a terrorist or a freedom fighter may have nothing to do with who they are but more to do with which side we are on. Similarly, what distinguishes a "religion" from a "cult"? Usually, a "cult" is a religion that someone doesn't like. Whether we call Scientology a religion or a cult probably depends on whether we like Scientology or not. When we use normative concepts like this, we appear to be stating matters of fact: "Scientology is a cult" or "these people are terrorists." However, in fact we may be just passing off our value judgments *as if* they were matters of fact (and, it turns out, value judgments are never matters of fact).

Many of these taxonomic distinctions also influence American law, which is another common theme that the authors repeatedly address in this book. American laws, particularly Supreme Court decisions, weigh heavily on what counts as American religion. The courts define religion, they legislate religious freedom issues, and they reach legal decisions that impact issues seemingly tangentially related to religion. Gay marriage, LGBTQIA+ issues, religion in/ and the workplace, abortion, birth control, and the limits of religious freedom are some of the issues impacted by the courts' decisions. These are some of the politically and culturally charged issues with increasingly partisan and polarized positions on both sides of related debates. When courts decide *this* practice deserves "religious freedom" protections, while *that* practice does not—because it's not religious—courts dictate winners and losers (and perhaps pass off judges' value judgments as if they were simply matters of fact). They tend to mollify winners and motivate losers to lobby for reform.

We found that when our students think about issues related to court decisions, they often process these decisions and their consequences through the theoretical lenses framed by clichés. Why can't religion be separate from politics? Why do Christians disagree with gay people? Why can't people practice religion in private? These are some of the common ideas that our students use to make intellectual sense of court decisions, but as this volume's contributors repeatedly argue, these are clichés that limit our students' ability to understand and to make intellectual sense of these issues. Many of the chapters in this book use court decisions and American laws to identify some of these more common clichés and to demonstrate the ways they limit our ability to think critically about complex issues and concerns.

As we talked to our students about court decisions and so-called culture war issues, we noticed a recurring theme where many of them drew a distinction between so-called progressive and conservative politics and where they assumed that the former had, first, the best terms and theories for understanding and theorizing political and religious issues, and second, the best solutions for rectifying these problems. As critically minded scholars, however, we identified that many of these students relied on clichés that silenced their critics and that naturalized their opinions as objective fact. It is often assumed that conservative religious traditions cling to the past—refusing to evolve or adjust to changing times—in part because that is sometimes how conservative groups describe themselves. For instance, in the first couple of decades of the twentieth century, some Christians identified themselves as fundamentalists, claiming that there were five, unchanging, fundamental tenets to Christianity: the fact that the Bible is without error, the claim that Jesus was divine, the claim that Jesus was born of a virgin, the claim that Jesus was resurrected from the dead, and the claim that Jesus will someday return. Much like the orientalist stereotype of Asian monks living on mountaintops and holding on to ancient traditions that are the same as they were thousands of years ago, these fundamentalists portrayed themselves as stuck in the past. The problem with the orientalist stereotype is that Asian monasteries are constantly changing in response to changing social, political, and cultural traditions (if you want proof, google "Buddhist monks using computers," and you will find lots of evidence that such monks don't reflect the stereotypes seen in films about the "mystic East"). Similarly, the Christian fundamentalists were not stuck in the past but were also changing in response to changing social, political, and cultural traditions. As is self-evident given even a cursory review of Christian doctrine across the last two centuries, Christians did not emphasize the claim that the Bible was without error until the nineteenth century. The church fathers themselves—see the writings of Origin, for instance—claimed that *of course* there are falsehoods and inaccuracies in the Bible. Even "fundamentalists" are changing with the times, even if they outright deny it. If we are going to produce scholarship that is worth being taken seriously, we cannot let our stereotypes about a group—or the stereotypes they produce about themselves—guide our scholarly studies.

In this volume, we asked several of the contributors to address these clichés. In doing so, our goal is not to criticize our liberal students (any more than we'd criticize our conservative students); rather, we want to identify and highlight ways that all our students make partisan assumptions that are to large extents fueled by clichés. As such, the chapters in this volume repeatedly address clichés about religion that our more politically progressive students tend to embrace and perpetuate.

Consequently, as you read through the following chapters, keep in mind the following sorts of questions:

- Where do our stereotypes conflict with evidence? That is, are our claims about a particular group based on a tiny sample? Might our claims about a small subset of a group not fit the group as a whole?

- Do our stereotypes reflect *what we want to be true*, rather than what we actually have evidence for?

- Are the concepts, terms, or distinctions we're using embedded with normative associations or value judgments? When we use a particular distinction, are we doing so to implicitly praise or condemn a group, a belief, or a practice?

- If everyone accepted a particular stereotype, what social or political consequences might follow? What actions do our stereotypes encourage us to take?

- Do our stereotypes line up with a political ideology? That is, if you are liberal, do you hold the same stereotypes that other liberals tend to assume? If you are conservative, do you hold stereotypes that other conservatives accept? If so, why do our stereotypes line up with our political views? And what might we be missing, or what might we be unable to see because we're committed to a political ideology?

1

"Religion Is Personal and Not Subject to Government Regulation"

Savannah H. Finver

As SARS-Cov-2—better known as COVID-19—spread like wildfire throughout the United States in 2020, state and municipal governments across the country began to take emergency action to slow the spread of the deadly virus. Mask mandates, strict social distancing guidelines (encouraging people to stand six feet apart from each other when in public), and caps on the maximum number of guests allowed at social gatherings or in public buildings became commonplace in many states, especially those most densely populated and/ or closest to international travel hubs. Perhaps predictably, the public backlash toward these emergency measures was almost immediate. Memes and videos began popping up all over social media denouncing mask mandates not only as the curbing of individual freedoms by a government entity but also as a crime against God. Restrictions on indoor gatherings which impacted the programming of churches, temples, and other houses of worship led to multiple lawsuits across the nation, some of which quickly reached the US Supreme Court, in which leaders alleged that religious organizations were unfairly targeted for special restrictions in violation of the US Constitution. While state and local governments continuously stressed that they enacted these mandates in the service of public health, individual citizens retorted that mask-wearing was a personal matter, a choice made in conjunction with one's private religious beliefs which, they contend, should not be subject to government regulation.

While it should be duly noted that the factors which contributed to US citizens' reactions to the COVID-19 pandemic and the emergency measures put in place to slow the spread are various and complex, what is most interesting for our purposes is to highlight the rhetorical shift between government officials' emphasis on *public* health and individual citizens' emphasis on *personal* freedom. On the one hand, this shift makes the two arguments *fundamentally irreconcilable.* What we mean by that is that, a priori or by definition, measures which attempt to account for the public as a whole cannot take into account every individual or personal objection. Similarly, focusing attention on every citizen's individual needs or desires cannot account for the good of the whole. On the other hand, placing emphasis on the personal beliefs and freedoms of individual citizens in this case relies heavily on a familiar cliché for those of us who engage in the academic study of religion, especially those of us who focus on the US context; namely, that because religion is a private and personal matter, it cannot and should not be subject to any kind of government intervention or regulation.

This cliché consists of two key claims: first, that religion is private and personal, and second, that religion is not subject to government regulation. In what follows, I will address each portion of the cliché in turn. Because the claim that "religion is a private matter" has already been treated extensively in the first volume of *Stereotyping Religion*, I will only treat it briefly here (see Walsh 2017). I will then focus more extensively on the claim that governments should not intervene in or attempt to regulate religion. In this latter section, we shall examine the implications of including religion as an item of special protection in the US Constitution, diving into three key Supreme Court cases which consider the question of what kinds of activities and entities count for the purposes of protection as "religion." By way of conclusion, we will return to our initial example of COVID-19 regulations to demonstrate that not only are state and local governments frequently involved in regulating religious activities (and historically have been), but that this involvement is actually made *inevitable* by the very laws designed to protect religion.

Religion Is Private and Personal

At the beginning of the third chapter of his influential work *The Idea of the Holy*, German Lutheran theologian Rudolf Otto boldly claims that anyone who has never encountered a religious experience "is requested to read no farther; for it is not easy to discuss questions of religious psychology with one . . . who cannot recall any intrinsically religious feelings" (Otto 1958, 8). Otto's understanding of religion as "psychological," as "intrinsic," as a matter of one's "feelings" is not uncommon, especially in everyday use in American cultural contexts. Especially toward the end of the twentieth century, however, this notion of religion as private and internal, particularly as a matter of personal belief or experience, has been increasingly critiqued by religious studies scholars both within and outside of the American context. There are many reasons why terms such as "belief" and "experience" prove problematic for some scholars of religion. The first and most straightforward of these is that, simply put, because "beliefs" are thought to be held within people's minds, we do not currently (and may never) have the technology to empirically prove whether or not people in fact hold the beliefs they claim to. There aren't many convincing means by which we can definitively measure belief, and the data that we do have available to us from social-psychological studies actually suggest that people's actions don't always line up with their stated beliefs. As Craig Martin notes in his recent work *Discourse and Ideology* (2022, 176), "reporting belief appears, from an anthropological perspective, sometimes to serve social functions largely unrelated to the content of the reported beliefs." In other words, there are many reasons why someone might claim to hold a belief in God even if they don't. One example we might consider is how US presidents often end their speeches with the phrase "God bless America." Of course, we can't definitively rule out the possibility that any given president may use this phrase because he (and I use the pronoun "he" intentionally here because, at least at the time of this writing, the United States has yet to have a female president) sincerely believes in God and wants Him to bless the nation. On the other hand, though, we might also consider that "God bless America" is a useful rhetorical (or linguistic) tool, one which inspires feelings of nationalism and can help a president gain favor with the (majority Christian) public.

Another critique of the notion of religion as an essentially personal and private belief is more historical in nature. As Malory Nye notes in his chapter on belief in *Religion: The Basics* (2004), defining religion as centrally about belief carries a heavily Christian bias, and particularly a Protestant Christian bias at that. Many social groups that we would traditionally define as "World Religions" don't make reference to belief at all, but instead emphasize rituals and actions. Hinduism and Buddhism are the most frequently cited examples of traditions of this kind. Another, lesser-known example that students in introductory religion courses often struggle with is that some people who identify as Jewish also identify as atheist, as Steven Ramey points out in his chapter "Do All Religious Adherents Believe in the Concept of a Higher Power?" in *Religion in 5 Minutes* (2017). I've often found that students respond to this example by asking, "but how can you be Jewish if you don't *believe* in God?" One answer that people who identify as both Jewish and atheist will sometimes give is that, while they don't believe in God, they still practice many of the Jewish holiday rituals, hold the same moral or social values that they inherited from Jewish family members, and enjoy eating foods that are traditionally associated with Judaism. Another way people will sometimes phrase this is: "I'm culturally Jewish, but not religious." This response is interesting because it also assumes that religion is fundamentally about belief in a higher power, whereas rituals and actions count as something different, something "cultural."

If we know that there are social groups we call "religions" that don't center around the concept of belief, why do we still so often insist that religion is something private, internal, and personal, especially in the United States? As many religious studies scholars have shown[1], this particular view of religion is a product of the Protestant Reformation (sixteenth century) and the Enlightenment (seventeenth to eighteenth centuries), during which time a fundamental split emerged between Protestant and Catholic forms of Christianity. Interestingly for our purposes, as Robyn Faith Walsh notes in her chapter "Religion Is a Private Matter" (2017), a central topic of concern in this split, taking place shortly after the Spanish Inquisition, was how much legal authority governments should have over churches. These questions were further complicated with the emergence of Enlightenment thinkers such as John Locke, who were advocating the importance of individual rights and freedoms for (land-owning, male) citizens. As Tracy Fessenden notes in her article "The Nineteenth Century Bible Wars and the Separation of Church and State," what emerged during this time was a "Protestant understanding of religion—defined largely in terms of the sanctity of individual belief, presumed to lie beyond the coercive reach of government or other powers" (Fessenden 2005, 785). The general idea behind this understanding of religion was that, if religion could be relegated to the depths of the mind, to something intrinsic and internal—in short, to a matter of private belief—government entities would have a particularly difficult time regulating religion since, by definition, it was literally out-of-reach. And as Craig Martin notes in *Masking Hegemony*, this view of religion proved particularly useful in providing a space for relatively harmless dissent. Citizens were supposedly free to *think* and *believe* whatever they wanted, just as long as their *actions* and *behaviors* never interrupted the status quo.

Years of repetition inevitably solidified this view of religion as a matter of personal belief in the minds of the American public, and it seems to be this definition of religion that informed the incorporation of the First Amendment into the US Constitution. Indeed, it was this very notion of religion as private belief that lent credence to the perceived "wall of separation" between church and state in the United States. And yet, with the large number of lawsuits that wind their way through the courts each year which allege First Amendment violations, we might well ask if such a wall truly does exist.

As evidenced by the recent COVID-19 restrictions, we could point out that, actually, the government seems very involved in matters of religion. Which buildings count as churches for purposes of tax exemptions? What kinds of holiday displays or monuments are considered "religious" as opposed to "historical" or "traditional"? When are certain ritual practices, such as animal sacrifice or the use of certain mind-altering substances, allowed to take place per freedom of religious exercise? What forms of marriage are protected by religious free exercise law? When is the refusal to bake a same-sex couple a wedding cake a matter of "private religious belief" or a public display of discrimination? These questions, and many others about what should qualify as "religion" under the First Amendment, have been at the center of US case law for much of the nation's history. With this in mind, it is to the second part of our cliché, "religion is not subject to government regulation," which we now turn.

Religion Is Not Subject to Government Regulation

The First Amendment to the US Constitution states, in pertinent part, "Congress shall make no law respecting an establishment of religion, or prohibiting the free exercise thereof" (U.S. Const. Amend. I). The two components of this portion of the Amendment are typically referred to as the Establishment Clause and the Free Exercise Clause. In theory, the Establishment Clause prevents the federal government from *establishing* or legitimating one religion to be followed by everyone in the nation, whereas the Free Exercise Clause prevents the federal government from interfering with individuals' free *exercise* or practice of the rituals and behaviors associated with their tradition. In an oversimplified reading of these clauses, we might say that the Establishment Clause seems designed to protect religious *belief*, while the Free Exercise Clause is designed to protect *practice* or *action*. Indeed, this seems to be the way the First Amendment is interpreted by the majority of the American public.

And yet, we would be remiss not to point out that the First Amendment seems deceptively simple on its face while remaining quite complex in its implications. It should first be noted that this Amendment, ratified along with the rest of the Bill of Rights on December 15, 1791, *only* applied to the federal government, *not* to the governments of individual states or municipalities. It was only Congress, made up of the Senate and the House of Representatives, who could not pass legislation establishing a national religion or limiting free exercise. This limit was seemingly resolved by the incorporation of the

Fourteenth Amendment on July 9, 1868, which states in pertinent part that "[n]o State shall make or enforce any law which shall abridge the privileges or immunities of citizens of the United States" (U.S. Const. Amend. XIV). Put simply, the Fourteenth Amendment made it illegal for individual states to adopt laws which contradicted the freedoms guaranteed to citizens by the federal government in the form of the Constitution.

Another less overt but equally important difficulty in interpreting and enacting the Establishment and Free Exercise Clauses is that the term "religion" is not defined anywhere in the Constitution; in fact, the only place that "religion" appears in the document is in the text of the First Amendment. This may not seem like a particularly problematic oversight at first glance. After all, most of us probably think we already know what religion is, or at least have a good sense about what counts. In his book *Before Religion* (2013), Brent Nongbri describes this sense of "knowing" as the "I know it when I see it" approach, wherein both scholars and the public have a difficult time articulating precisely what they mean by the term "religion," but seem to have no trouble identifying which groups or activities should be identified as such (Nongbri 2013, 15–16). Willi Braun describes this phenomenon a bit differently in *The Guide to the Study of Religion* (2000) when he writes that "[a]s a specter, 'religion' presents us with the dual problem of being flamboyantly real, meeting us in all forms of speech and in material representations, on the one hand, and frustratingly apt to turn coy or disintegrate altogether when put under inquisition, on the other" (Braun 2000, 3–4). What I take Braun here to mean is that we're confronted with phenomena which are identified as "religious"—things like churches, temples, and mosques; prayers; special kinds of clothing or accessories like yarmulkes, rosaries, or hijabs; and various symbols of religion like crosses, six-pointed stars, or depictions of Hindu deities in meditation poses—all the time in our daily lives, but when it comes time to reach a consensus about what the term "religion" actually means, and which groups should definitively count, we seem to have some trouble agreeing.

Designating religion as an object of special protection in an official document like the Constitution without defining it raises legal complications on at least two fronts. First, by singling religion out as an object of privileges and protections, the First and Fourteenth Amendments paradoxically force federal, state, and local governments to become involved in matters of regulation by definition. It's the responsibility of bureaucratic federal agencies such as the Internal Revenue Service (IRS), for example, to determine which organizations should qualify as "religious" for the purposes of granting tax exemption status. Complicating questions of tax exemption even further, the status normally granted to religious groups, the 501(c)(3) designation, can actually be granted to *any* charitable organization, private foundation, or nonprofit group as long as they meet the requirements designated by the IRS.

Thus, even if a nonreligious charitable group is granted 501(c)(3) tax exemption status, they may be seen as a religious organization by members of the public who are unfamiliar with the intricacies of tax law. Similarly, groups that apply for recognition under the 501(c)(3) exemption may be identified by the IRS as public or private charities or nonprofits even if the group itself identifies as religious (see especially the "Exempt Organization Types" page of the IRS official website). This very complication caused quite a stir in 2019 when an infamous Satanic group known as The Satanic Temple (TST) filed for and was granted 501(c)(3) exemption status. Though the letter delivered to TST on behalf of the IRS specifically designates the group as a "public charity," a strong backlash ensued in the media with many declaring that a Satanic group can't be a real religion and shouldn't be officially recognized as such by the US government (see Bell 2019; Dickson 2019). Perhaps those voices behind the backlash were unaware at the time of how frequently TST had filed lawsuits, with various local- and state-level courts claiming violations of both the Establishment and Free Exercise Clauses, and lost their cases (Laycock 2020).

The struggles that TST faced in their various lawsuits bring us to the second legal issue that the lack of an official definition of "religion" raises. Because questions about what kinds of groups and behaviors should count as properly religious for civil rights purposes are almost always hashed out in local, state, and federal courts, the various judges and justices are more or less left to their own devices when deciding which groups and individuals should qualify and under what conditions. While it is true that the courts are supposed to rely on legal precedent (meaning the case law which came before) when making these decisions, it must be said that *there can be no precedent* for newly emerging groups identifying as religious and also that which cases count as precedent can change over time. We will explore the idea of changing legal precedents shortly, but for the moment, the most important takeaway is that which groups and individuals qualify for protections and privileges are often left up to judges' personal opinions about what exactly the term "religion" means and/or refers to.

The preeminent scholar of religion and law, Winnifred Fallers Sullivan, makes this point well in her book *The Impossibility of Religious Freedom* (2005), in which she provides a detailed examination of the case of *Warner v. Boca Raton* (1999). The central question at play in the *Warner* case was whether or not individual citizens should be allowed to display religious symbols at burial sites that were privately purchased but placed on public land. Yet, which symbols count as religious, as special, as deserving of protection, as opposed to secular, not religious, not deserving of special protections? Sullivan argues that, for the judge involved in the *Warner* case, Judge Ryskamp, which symbols counted as religious were based largely on *his own understanding of the definition of religion.* She writes that Ryskamp "for his part, in his opinions and in his questions, was not deferential to religious authority, whether clerical or academic"—and we might well ask here who or what gets to count as a "religious authority" (2005, 133). Sullivan elaborates:

> You could hear him thinking out loud as he developed his own theory of religion. [. . .] With each expert Ryskamp tried to work out his own view of what religion is and what particular religious traditions demand of their adherents with respect to burial. You could also see him working, however, from within what is a basically Protestant understanding of authority. It is the individual who decides. And he does so by reading the Bible. (Sullivan 2005, 133)

As I have already illustrated, the notion of religion as private and individual is a distinctly Protestant idea, and it's a pervasive view in the United States. Thus, when judges are left to their own discretion in defining religion, it's perhaps not all that surprising that they often fall back on Protestant definitions (whether they recognize those ideas as Protestant or not) when determining *whose* beliefs and actions should really be protected and privileged by a court of law.

The very act of defining religion in this way, through the legal machine of the courts, makes it fundamentally regulatory in nature. We don't have a specific, static, unchanging definition of religion in the law. While some people likely interpret this flexibility as a positive feature, in point of fact it actually provides legal and government actors with *more* regulatory power and extensive possibilities for intervention into the lives (and sometimes the very bodies—we should think here, especially, of the recent overturning of *Roe v. Wade* [1973] in the Supreme Court case *Dobbs v. Jackson* [2022]) of citizens. Without a concrete definition, these questions about who and what counts as "religious" in a legal context will be—and always have been—up for debate, continuously granting courts the opportunity to potentially restrict or otherwise reinvent the definition anew. This is why Sullivan ultimately concludes that "religious freedom," at least in the sense of complete freedom of the individual to believe what they wish and to act according to those beliefs, is impossible to attain by way of granting special protections and privileges to religion. She notes that "[w]hen law claims authority over religion, even for the purpose of ensuring its freedom, lines must be drawn" (Sullivan 2005, 148). "Religion," Sullivan writes, "is not limitlessly free in any human society, even in the United States" (2005, 155).

But we need not take Sullivan's word for it; any detailed examination of US case law which centers on questions of establishment or free exercise will inevitably lead us to similar conclusions. Consider, for example, the first US Supreme Court Case on the subject of free exercise, *Reynolds v. United*

States (1878). George Reynolds was a member of the Church of Jesus Christ of Latter-Day Saints, commonly known as the Mormon Church. The main issue of the case revolved around the fact that Reynolds, allegedly in accordance with his religious beliefs, had taken a second wife while his first wife was still living, in direct violation of an established federal law, the Morrill Anti-Bigamy Act of 1862. At trial, Reynolds claimed that the Anti-Bigamy Act violated the Free Exercise Clause of the First Amendment, since his religion expressly directed him that it was his sacred duty to practice polygamy. Yet, in a unanimous opinion, the justices of the Supreme Court disagreed. They write in their opinion that "the question is raised whether religious belief can be accepted as a justification of an overt act made criminal by the law of the land" (*Reynolds*, 98 U.S. 145, 162 [1878]). To answer this question, the Court first turned to language in the Constitution, which they explicitly acknowledge does not offer a definition of religion for the Court to rely upon (*Reynolds*, 163 [1878]). Because of this lack of a clear definition, the Court then decided that they must look elsewhere to determine the scope of the protections guaranteed by the First Amendment.

The *Reynolds* Court ultimately leaned heavily on the work of the former US president Thomas Jefferson to determine how they should interpret the First Amendment, noting that Jefferson had played a major role in the framing of the Constitution and the later adoption of the Bill of Rights. Following a lengthy quotation from a letter which Jefferson had written to the Danbury Baptist Association (and we may well note here that this letter was not a legal document; in other words, it bore no official weight other than the preference given to it by the *Reynolds* Court), the Court writes:

> Coming as [the letter] does from an acknowledged leader of the advocates of the measure, it may be accepted almost as an authoritative declaration of the scope and effect of the amendment thus secured. Congress was deprived of all legal power over *mere opinion*, but was left free to reach *actions* which were in violation of social duties or subversive of good order. (*Reynolds*, 164 [1878]; my emphasis)

The implication here is that, while the justices have determined that they can't stop Reynolds from *believing* that living in a polygamous marriage is his sacred duty, they can nonetheless prevent him from *acting* on those beliefs, so long as they interpret those actions as an immediate threat to the moral order of the nation. Indeed, in the very next paragraph of the opinion, the Court writes that "[p]olygamy has always been odious among the northern and western nations of Europe, and, until the establishment of the Mormon Church, was almost exclusively a feature of the life of Asiatic and of African people" (*Reynolds*, 164 [1878]). Interestingly, the Court offers no evidence to support this rather sweeping generalization; they seem to be relying here on overtly racist assumptions to denigrate polygamy by associating it with cultures and locations that were commonly viewed as "savage" during the nineteenth century as a result of colonial expansion. Having defined polygamy as "odious," as a "crime," it no longer seems to matter that polygamy is required by the tenants of Reynolds' religion. Polygamy is made to be a social disruption first and a religious ritual only secondarily, if at all. In this way, the Court authorizes its own regulatory power over what actions qualify as "religious" for the purposes of free exercise.

Let us consider another example. The case of *Employment Division, Department of Human Resources of Oregon v. Smith* (1990) was decided some 110 years after the *Reynolds* case but bears some important resemblances. Brought to the courts by Alfred Smith and Galen Black, the *Smith* case focused on the question of whether the state of Oregon could deny unemployment benefits to the two men following their dismissal from their jobs as counselors at a drug rehabilitation facility. The reason for the dismissal was that Smith and Black had ingested peyote as part of a religious ritual at the Native American Church. Peyote was considered an illegal substance in Oregon, but as in the *Reynolds* case, Smith and Black alleged that being denied unemployment benefits by the Department of Human Resources abridged their First Amendment right to free exercise. Supreme Court Justice Antonin Scalia, writing the opinion for the 6-3 majority, disagreed. Once again emphasizing the distinction between *belief* and *action*, Scalia writes:

> But the "exercise of religion" often involves not only belief and profession but the *performance* of (or abstention from) physical acts: assembling with others for a worship service, participating in sacramental use of bread and wine, proselytizing, abstaining from certain foods or certain modes of transportation. It would be true, we think (though no case of ours has involved the point), that a state would be "prohibiting the free exercise [of religion]" if it sought to ban such acts or abstentions only when they are engaged in for religious reasons, or only because of the religious belief that they display. (*Employment Division v. Smith*, 494 U.S. 872, 877 [1990]; my emphasis)

Scalia's main argument here is that laws which have been written to *target* specific religious behaviors or actions—such as a law making the receiving of communion illegal, for example—would be considered a violation of the First Amendment right to free exercise. Crucially for Scalia's argument, though, the Oregon law in question was allegedly not designed to target the Native American Church specifically; rather, the law is "generally applicable" in that it makes peyote use illegal across all of Oregon *regardless* of a person's individual religious beliefs. This is a very similar argument to the one we saw earlier in the *Reynolds* case, which held that because polygamy was banned across the United States by federal law, it was not targeting Reynolds' religious beliefs, but instead an action he took that was known at the time to be "odious" and disruptive of public order. As we have already seen, the Supreme Court seems to view the regulation of behaviors and actions as well within the purview of the federal government.

One important difference between the *Reynolds* case and the *Smith* case is that the *Reynolds* decision was issued by a *unanimous* court whereas the *Smith* case contains a dissenting opinion. Unanimous decisions presented by the Supreme Court are somewhat rare and are often utilized to discourage the public from bringing similar cases in the future to contest the Court's opinion. As we may recall, earlier in this section, I raised the issue of shifting legal precedent. We now have occasion to return to this issue as the dissenting opinion in the *Smith* case rests upon this very question. In the years between *Reynolds* and *Smith*, many cases (the most important of which were *Sherbert v. Verner* [1963] and *Wisconsin v. Yoder* [1972]) reached the Supreme Court in which the *Reynolds* decision was contested and reevaluated. During this time, the Supreme Court had repeatedly concluded, as Justice O'Connor writes in his dissent to *Smith*:

> [W]e [the Court] have respected both the First Amendment's express textual mandate and the governmental interest in regulation of conduct by requiring the Government to justify any substantial burden on religiously motivated conduct by a compelling state interest and by means narrowly tailored to achieve that interest. (*Smith*, 894 [1990])

The "compelling state interest" argument that O'Connor raises here—that is, the argument that a generally applicable law can restrict free exercise rights *only* if the state has shown that the law is absolutely required to maintain public order—had been considered the foundational legal precedent until Scalia, in the *Smith* case, reverted to *Reynolds* as a more applicable standard. The *Smith* case therefore demonstrates to us that the lack of firm definitions and standards in the language of the First Amendment grants the Supreme Court—and by extension, the federal government—a great deal of flexibility in how extensive their regulation over religious action can be.

Let us consider one final example with slightly different circumstances than the *Reynolds* and *Smith* cases. As you may have already noted, the two cases we have just explored both involved minority religious traditions: Mormonism and the Native American Church. We have also noted that the plaintiffs in both of these cases were unsuccessful at securing what they saw as their constitutional right to free exercise. Our next case, *Burwell v. Hobby Lobby*

Stores (2014), still centers on questions of religious free exercise, but this time, the owners of the Hobby Lobby chain are part of a majority religious tradition in the United States, Christianity, and as we will shortly see, they were successful in securing their free exercise rights. The primary question in this case almost sounds a little silly upon first hearing it: can closely held, for-profit companies be considered to hold "religious beliefs" for the purposes of free exercise law? If you're wondering how a corporation or a business can hold anything like a religious belief without a consciousness, you wouldn't be the only one; indeed, the dissenting opinion for the case asks just such a question. Writing for a 5-4 majority, however, Justice Samuel A. Alito, Jr., argued that, since closely held corporations are generally owned and operated by one family, businesses like Hobby Lobby can be said to have "religious beliefs" because the family that owns them likely runs their business in accordance with those beliefs.

Why did it matter for the purposes of this case whether or not a corporation could hold religious beliefs? The Green family, which owns the Hobby Lobby chain, had been denying female employees insurance coverage for certain types of contraceptives that the Greens saw as "abortifacients," that is, medications like Plan B, which the Greens thought could induce an abortion. Interestingly, though it is never mentioned in the opinion of the case, the Food and Drug Administration (FDA) seems to disagree. In his article "The Corporately Produced Conscience: Emergency Contraception and the Politics of Workplace Accommodations," Isaac Weiner (2017) addresses this point through his analysis of the *Hobby Lobby* case when he writes, "Although it is technically not an abortifacient, Plan B has been described as such by many religious conservatives in the United States—whether out of ignorance, political calculation, or sincere belief." In this case, "both the majority and dissent accepted the 'sincerity' of Hobby Lobby's owners' beliefs regarding Plan B's abortifacient properties, even if factually incorrect according to medical science," and it was on the basis of this "sincerity" that the court ultimately reached its ruling: closely held corporations *can* hold religious beliefs, and those beliefs need to be protected to the full extent of the law regardless of whether scientific discourses have determined them to be false (Weiner 2017, 33).

This conclusion seems to be a stark contrast to the *Reynolds* and *Smith* decisions, in which none of the plaintiffs were successful in securing free exercise rights to practice their own rituals. One rather simple explanation is that the *Hobby Lobby* Court was different from the other Courts. Different justices were sitting on the bench in all three cases, and as we've already explored, what counts as "religion" in these cases is largely left up to individual justices to determine. Another possible explanation is that the *Reynolds* and *Smith* cases are obvious examples of discrimination against minorities. It doesn't seem like much of an accident that a self-identifying Mormon and two indigenous men were denied free exercise rights when both groups have experienced near constant misrepresentation and often outright hostility throughout US history, while a white, Christian family was able to navigate the Court system to their own advantage in a way that severely restricted the decisions that their female employees could make about their bodies. Even if discrimination against minorities turned out to be the result of these cases, however, I'm inclined to believe that a complete explanation is more complex than either of the previous conclusions would demonstrate. For example, one complication we might note is that the Court became increasingly divided in their opinions for each case, from unanimity to a narrow 5-4 majority. This increasing divide indicates, to my mind at least, that public and political ideas about what kinds of groups, beliefs, and behaviors should qualify for protections under the First Amendment have been shifting, even if only slightly, over time. More importantly, though, what the general public and sometimes even scholars seem to fail to take into account is that the phrasing of the First Amendment lends itself to ever-increasing government oversight.

At least one former US president, James Madison, recognized this potentiality before the Bill of Rights was ratified. In his Memorial and Remonstrance of 1785, Madison made it plain that he thought the federal government should stay out of matters of religion altogether, neither establishing a privileged state religion nor granting religion special rights. David Sehat notes of Madison in his book *The Myth of American Religious Freedom* (2011) that Madison "recognized that majorities could use their access to government to suppress and tyrannize minorities. Therefore, the rights of the minority had to be protected from the will of the majority" (36). In Madison's view, the only way to do this effectively would be to guarantee individual rights to all citizens. But the First Amendment doesn't guarantee any particular rights to any particular individual. Recall the precise phrasing of the Amendment: "Congress shall make no law respecting an establishment of religion, or prohibiting the free exercise thereof." At no point in any of the three cases explored in the chapter did Congress or any state legislature pass a law which strictly prohibited or targeted religious free exercise, even if a limit to free exercise *turned out to be the result*. The (perhaps intendedly) vague nature of the language of the First Amendment itself brought Madison's fears to life. As it turns out, leaving religion undefined in the Constitution not only invites government oversight; it also places minorities (whether as groups or individuals) at a disadvantage when seeking the protection of the law.

Conclusion

In closing, then, let us return to the cliché with which we opened our chapter: "Religion Is Personal and Not Subject to Government Regulation." In the first section, I argued that religion as a matter of private or personal belief is only one particular, Protestant-informed notion; most groups identifying as "religions" have some form of rituals or behaviors which cannot be reduced to the merely personal. In the second section, I argued that the language of the First Amendment itself invites government regulation both by leaving "religion" undefined and by making religion, at the same time, an object of special protection. We have found, through our exploration of the *Reynolds*, *Smith*, and *Hobby Lobby* cases, that government regulation often, but not always, has a disproportional impact on minority groups. Thus, we might say that the view captured by our cliché, while pervasive in American popular culture, obscures more than it explains.

Returning, then, to our initial example of COVID-19 restrictions, we might say that the very notion of these public safety measures infringing on religious beliefs and practices rests upon a host of problematic assumptions about what exactly the First Amendment says (and doesn't say), what and who it was designed to protect, and how those protections play out in the American legal sphere. It has never been suggested in any free exercise case that federal and state governments are not well within their rights to regulate their citizens' behaviors and actions, especially when enacting laws that the government feels are in service of the protection of the public as a whole. We might even go so far as to say that both the COVID-19 restrictions themselves and the backlash against them are just a rehashing of the same familiar disagreements which are a direct result of how the First Amendment is written. Far from indicating a failing on behalf of the legal system in the United States, our current moment (at the time of this writing) is an example of the law functioning *as it was intended to*. It is also a firm reminder of all of the assumptions we carry when we claim not only that our religious beliefs belong to us alone but that the government doesn't (or shouldn't) have the power to regulate us.

2

"Religious Freedom Is about Religious Freedom"

Rita Lester and Jacob Barrett

Religious freedom is often called The First Freedom in a reference to both its position in the First Amendment of the US Constitution and its assumed importance above all other freedoms guaranteed to US citizens.[1] Although it can be claimed socially and informally, appeals to religious freedom are commonly made by politicians, religious leaders, and other public figures to advocate for or against very public issues like health care and civil rights. Employers, schools, and prisons all allow for formal religious freedom claims and provide a special process for accommodation or exception. We see (increasingly so, it seems) contests of religious freedom in the news where a person, organization, or corporation wants to do something—or not do something—that is expected of the general population. In 2017, a Kentucky county clerk refused to sign marriage licenses for same-sex couples claiming doing so went against her religious beliefs. In 2019, a person challenged Missouri's anti-abortion law claiming that her right to religious freedom included the right to bodily autonomy.[2] But just because something is claimed as religious freedom does not mean it is granted. For example, both of the previously mentioned individuals lost their cases.

Even though we know not all things people call "religion" or "religious" are allowed under the law, we commonly assume religious freedom to be a clear and obvious thing that protects the rights of individuals to believe and practice in accordance with their religion. When people of every political stripe talk about religious freedom this way, it distracts from and covers up how religious freedom in US law works to manage what gets to count as religion or religious and, therefore, what does not. Practically speaking, "religious freedom" refers to a cluster of assertions, policies, and pieces of legislation that allow or disallow exemptions based on claims that something is religious.[3] Religious reasons for or against doing something are treated as special in US law and the outcomes, whether brief social skirmishes or years-long court cases, have material implications that redistribute power and resources. Rulings on religious freedom define, and in turn create, what gets to count as religion by approving and disapproving requests by the person or organization bringing such a claim. This means that the government is always in the business of defining religion and so strict separation, or what Thomas Jefferson called a "high wall" of separation, between church and state is impossible.[4] If, as Bruce Lincoln suggests, religion is a discourse that claims transcendent authority, then social and legal outcomes illuminate the plasticity of the "religious" in religious freedom.[5]

Much writing on religious freedom is about whether court decisions are right or wrong, or how religious freedom can be improved upon and better realized. In this book, instead of promoting or defending the concept under consideration, we are examining where it comes from, how it works, and what is uncovered if we read against the popular assumptions. It is more popular, upon hearing a claim of religious freedom, to pivot to judgments about whether the person or organization making the religious freedom claim is sincere or authentic by asking questions like "Is the person *really* religious? Is it a *real* religion?" Instead, let's examine the taken-for-grantedness of both the object and the subject of religious freedom, that is, *the what* (what gets to count) and *the who* (who gets to claim it). In doing so, we find out that both *the what* and *the who* are always changing.

Putting the Religious in Religious Freedom: An Origin Story

Our origin story of religious freedom begins in sixteenth- and seventeenth-century Europe. Earlier, religion and state were not understood or treated as separate spheres. Starting in the sixteenth-century Protestant Reformations, Protestant groups began rejecting Catholicism's emphasis on (what Protestants considered to be) "insincere" ritual and practice. The prime example of this is Martin Luther's argument that people's inner conscience is the location of authentic religion. Luther's, and more broadly Protestantism's, rejection of Catholic devotion to ritual minimized religion to a set of internally held beliefs.

The United States inherited this habit of thinking of religion as private and individual when early influential figures in the nation's development successfully advocated against the establishment of a state religion. Eighteenth- and nineteenth-century colonial and presidential figures such as William Penn, Thomas Jefferson, and James Madison took strong stances for religious freedom against establishing a state religion, citing a wide range of reasons from tyranny to the offensive nature of suggesting that Christianity needed state affiliation to thrive.[6] While these arguments are ones we are familiar with today, the idea of a nation without a state religion was something new at the time. Without a state religion, religious liberty was created and understood in a way that it had not been before. This resistance to an established state religion and the spread of religious freedom furthered and reinforced the idea that religion was a personal, private set of beliefs. Religious freedom was born out of the specific context of early modern Europe's ideas about religion informing the ideas of influential figures in the formation of the United States. Today, this legacy continues and is seen in the popular views that people hold their beliefs in their hearts and religion is more about a personal attitude or spiritual experience than it is about organized, communal practices.

In US society and law today, religious freedom is shorthand for one of the two parts of the First Amendment to the US Constitution. Scholars call the first part the Establishment Clause ("Congress shall make no law respecting an establishment of religion"), because it is understood to prohibit state sponsorship of religion. Scholars call the second part the Free Exercise Clause ("or prohibiting the free exercise thereof"), because it is understood to protect religion from government interference. Federal, state, and local laws manage religion in thousands of mundane ways (zoning for buildings, marriage licenses, educational calendars, taxes, etc.) and each decision defines "religious" in certain ways, reinforcing, regulating, and supporting the power or behavior of some and not others.

Since religious freedom is the cumulation of legislation managing religious difference, what gets to count as the "religious" in religious freedom is always changing. This managing of religious difference is built on culturally constructed distinctions between good religion (protected) and bad or not-religion (not protected). These distinctions, more times than not, shake out as "good" being synonymous with "looking like Western, Protestant Christianity" and "bad" meaning "looking different" or "doing things not considered necessary in Protestant Christianity." As J. Brent Crosson points out, religion-making includes creating and maintaining a distinction between "harmless/good religion" and "harmful/bad religion" (or not-religion) as a way to limit and distribute rights, citizenship, and freedom (see Crosson 2020).

What follows is an exploration of two famous, but different, US Supreme Court cases that complicate the common cliché that religious freedom is about the guaranteed rights for individuals to practice their religion in accordance with their personal beliefs. These cases demonstrate how religious freedom is a strategy for defining and redefining what is "religious," what is not, and who or what gets to claim it. The first case, *Church of the Lukumi Babalu Aye v. City of Hialeah* (1993), concerns a religious minority suing their city council for the right to do something. The second case, *Burwell v. Hobby Lobby Stores, Inc.* (2014), concerns a for-profit retail corporation refusing to do something employers were required to do by law. In both cases, "religion" and "religious" were renegotiated in ways that unsettle the stereotypical cliché of religion as personal, private beliefs and complicate *the what* and *the who* of religious freedom.

The What: It's Not about the Chickens

The Supreme Court case *Church of the Lukumi Babalu Aye v. City of Hialeah* (1993) provides an excellent example of how, even when religious freedom is designed to benefit the dominant group, a minority religion can leverage religious freedom claims, renegotiating what gets to count as "religion" and "religious." The case centered a dispute between a Cuban Santeria group and the town council of Hialeah (a town located within Miami-Dade County, Florida) over the issue of animal sacrifice. Following Fidel Castro's rule after the Cuban revolution, there was a mass exodus of Cuban citizens who settled in southern Florida. Santeria, an Afro-Caribbean religion fusing Catholicism and Yoruba, came to Florida with the immigrants and by the 1980s had amassed between 50,000 and 100,000 followers in the state. In 1974, Ernesto Pichardo cofounded the Church of the Lukumi Babalu Aye and for over a decade led the Santeria group in Hialeah without a brick-and-mortar meeting space. Pichardo announced in 1987 the group's plan to open a physical church that would act not only as a place for the group to hold rituals and perform animal sacrifices but also as a museum and cultural center for the community. Almost immediately, the group was met with intense pushback from other religious groups and civic organizations over their plans to sacrifice chickens as part of their religious rituals.[7] Santeria uses the sacrificing of chickens as a fundamental part of their ceremonies and community building, claiming the animal's life force feeds the orishas (ancestral spirits) with food either being left for the orishas (sometimes in public places) or consumed by the community.

Protests over the group's use of animals slaughtering/sacrifice ranged from concerns about animal abuse to satanic worship to the psychological trauma on children. On June 9, 1987, the town council held a hearing at which they passed an emergency ordinance and resolution that focused on the cruelty of animal sacrifice. Following their June meeting, the council passed three additional ordinances in September that criminalized animal sacrifices for ritual purposes. While the ordinances banned the ritual sacrificing of animals, the council made special exemptions for slaughterhouses (Jewish kashrut/kosher and commercial), hunting, fishing, killing of stray animals, and feeding rabbits to racing greyhounds.

By doing this, Hialeah put ordinances into effect banning animal sacrifice within city limits in what Pichardo claimed was a targeted attack on the religious liberties of the Santeria group. Pichardo challenged the city ordinance in the courts, first suing the council in the United States District Court for the Southern District of Florida. Following a ruling in favor of the council, Pichardo appealed and received another unfavorable ruling in the US Court of Appeals for the Eleventh Circuit. In 1993, he took his case against the city of Hialeah, Florida, to the Supreme Court of the United States (SCOTUS) on the grounds that the city's ordinances against animal sacrifice violated the church's freedom of exercise rights.

Pichardo's case was accepted by the Supreme Court and would become a landmark case in religious freedom. The legal team for the Church argued that the ordinances had singled out Santeria, arguing that "what they've done here is say, you can kill animals for almost any reason—just because you're tired of taking care of them, that's a good enough reason. That's necessary—but not for religious reasons." The attorney for Hialeah argued that the city simply banned the practice of ritual animal sacrifice and was not banning Santeria beliefs. The Supreme Court sided with Pichardo, clarifying that "The Free Exercise Clause commits government itself to religious tolerance, and upon even slight suspicions that proposals for state intervention stem from animosity to religion or distrust of its practices, all officials must pause to remember their own high duty to the Constitution and the rights it secures" (for a detailed account of this case, see O'Brien 2004).

What we can see in the Hialeah case is that the "religious" in religious freedom is not static. In this decision, SCOTUS extended religious freedom from beliefs to practices, contrary to a ruling from 1879 that set the precedent for prioritizing beliefs and not practices.[8] When SCOTUS ruled in favor of Pichardo, it redefined "religion" and "religious freedom" to include action in a way it had not before. We know from earlier in this chapter that the assumption that religion is a personal, private set of beliefs is a context-specific understanding of religion that does not apply to other groups from other contexts. Until a group from a different context that had a different understanding of what religion looked like disrupted the system and drew attention, religious freedom did not *need* to include action. The Protestant Christian majority that had defined religion did not need religious freedom to include action because they did not benefit from that definition.

While today it is common to understand religious freedom in light of the Hialeah case, religious freedom did not always protect religious practice. What counts as protectable changes through the courts' redefining and renegotiation of "religion" and "religious." If we begin to complicate the idea that religious freedom is about guaranteeing the rights of individuals to believe and practice their religion freely with attention to how the courts are always defining and redefining what "religion" is and what is "religious," we can see how religious freedom claims function. In other words, when we challenge the idea that *the what* in religious freedom is clear and consistent, we begin to see the bigger work religious freedom claims are doing. Though on the surface the Hialeah case appears to be a matter of a group's right under the First Amendment to sacrifice chickens, it's not about the chickens. While the case was a win for a minority religious group against the dominant group—an outcome that is not often in religious freedom cases—the win represents something much more than granting rights to a marginal group. As Pichardo's case rose to the Supreme Court, it garnered the attention of many other groups that, when SCOTUS agreed to hear the case, submitted arguments for the court to consider. When that happened, the case was no longer about the Santeria group's right to kill chickens in Hialeah. Now, the case was about how SCOTUS was defining *the what* in religious freedom, which claims it would grant legitimacy to, and all of the groups that had a vested interest in the court redefining religion to include action.

The argument of this chapter is that religious freedom does not refer to a stable, obvious, identifiable thing. In the Hialeah case we saw a less known and less centralized plaintiff, the Church of Lukumi Babalu Aye, making and winning a claim for protection of a religious practice that redefined *the what* in religious freedom. Hialeah is a high-profile example of how even the typical interpretation of what counts as religious in religious freedom can change to include actions (not just beliefs), and the next case illustrates the changeable nature of who get to claim religious freedom. *Burwell v. Hobby Lobby Stores, Inc.* (2014), instead of protecting the private conscience of individuals, protects, instead, commercial corporations, shifting *the who* in religious freedom.

The Who: A Person's a Person, No Matter How Corporate

The more recent SCOTUS case *Burwell v. Hobby Lobby Stores, Inc.* (2014) redefined *the who* in who gets religious freedom by extending the First Amendment's protections of religious freedom to a for-profit corporation. Often when Americans think of religious freedom, many assume it to be the protection for an individual's free-range personal choice that, because it is religious, cannot be interfered with. This idea of religious freedom as individual protection, though, is limited. An example of how not all individuals get to be *the who* in religious freedom can be seen in *Employment Division v. Smith* (1989), where Native American Church (NAC) member Alfred Smith was fired and denied unemployment compensation for ingesting peyote. The NAC considers peyote a sacrament or medicine, but the US law classifies it a Schedule I controlled substance for its hallucinogenic qualities. When this case went before the Supreme Court in 1989, Smith, a member of the Klamath Nation of Oregon, lost.

Two things come out of Smith that are relevant to the Hobby Lobby case: what a SCOTUS Justice said about why he voted against Smith's religious freedom claim and the legislative response that was intended to protect religious minorities post-*Smith*. In 1990, Supreme Court Justice Antonin Scalia wrote that religious freedom does "not include violating existing state laws," that "an individual's religious beliefs do not give them an exception from complying with state laws," and, Scalia worried, about "open[ning] religious exemptions for all kinds of civic obligations from taxes, child welfare and labor laws, traffic laws, vaccination requirements, environmental protection, and laws providing equality" (see Urban 2015). Here, we see well-known conservative SCOTUS Justice Scalia defining religious freedom as *not* including an individual's right to gain exemption from things that are expected of everyone else.

The second relevant thing to note is that Smith's loss spurred a new piece of legislation, The Religious Freedom Restoration Act of 1993 (RFRA). RFRA was initially hailed as a victory for religious freedom, righting (what Congress and dissenting SCOTUS justices saw as) the wrong of the *Smith* outcome. The act sought to set stricter and clearer guidance for how the Court was to make decisions on a person's claim to the Free Exercise Clause of the First Amendment. The irony of RFRA, though, is that it continued to change *the who* of religious freedom in ways that work against the rights of individuals. In an attempt to pass legislation to correct for the ruling against Smith in the peyote case by protecting religious freedom for minoritized religions like the Native American Church, RFRAs have been used to protect a new kind of plaintiff, in a novel kind of exercise of religious freedom, over an issue (only) assumed to be religious.

In 2014, the Supreme Court took up a case that challenged who RFRA protects when it heard *Burwell v. Hobby Lobby Stores, Inc.* Under the Affordable Care Act (ACA), employers were required to offer health-care coverage in their insurance policies. Specifically, the ACA required employment-based group health-care plans to cover specific FDA-approved contraceptive methods. Hobby Lobby[9] did not want to provide coverage for what the ACA deemed essential health care, claiming that being required to provide their employees access to contraceptives was a burden on the corporation's exercise of religious freedom. Notice here that a corporation is the "person" claiming religious freedom. Barbara and David Green, the owners of the Hobby Lobby Corporation, sued the director of US Health and Human Services claiming that enforcement of the ACA's contraceptive mandate violated Hobby Lobby's free exercise of religion and, therefore, RFRA. In a 5-4 decision, SCOTUS ruled in favor of Hobby Lobby, affirming that the corporation could deny its employees' health-care contraceptive coverage—though three days later a government-sponsored alternative was established that would provide employees with no-cost contraceptives if their employer did not provide such coverage—because RFRA protected the corporation's free exercise of religion.

Although Hobby Lobby is owned by a Protestant, evangelical family that views contraception as immoral, the claim raised in this case was not the family's beliefs or their connection to any religious tradition, but the burden to the exercise of religious freedom of the corporation. The Greens claimed that allowing for contraception in the health-care plan for their employees would be against Hobby Lobby's exercise of religious freedom. In this case, Hobby Lobby wanted to extend the "private" beliefs of the owners to their corporation and, hence, their employees who may or may not have shared the Greens' views on contraception. Notice that individuals are not *the who* of religious freedom here. The case was not about the Greens' claiming religious freedom nor the employees raising issue with being denied access to the health care they were entitled to (as private citizens with private decisions to make about the seemingly private issues of reproduction). Instead, the for-profit national chain of retail craft sellers became *the who*, the "person," with standing before the law to claim that doing something required was against their (its?!) freedom of religious exercise. The Greens wanted to use their private beliefs to form (or inform) their company's policies and thus claiming an exemption to a public law that applied to every other organization like their own. That is, the public law that applied to everyone else did not apply to the Green's company because of their supposed "private" religious beliefs—which apparently had a great deal of "public" import despite their "private" status.

Though Hobby Lobby received a favorable ruling from SCOTUS, the outcome extends beyond just the right to deny their employees contraceptive health-care coverage. It won the right for a corporation to control (or ignore) the otherwise legal rights of their employees by making appeals to and receiving religious freedom exemptions to the law. By claiming that providing health-care coverage for contraceptives violated the corporation's exercise of religious freedom, the *Hobby Lobby* ruling shifted *the who* in religious freedom so it was no longer about individual conscience but instead about a corporation's (as a legal, fictive person) rights. When ruling in favor of Hobby Lobby, SCOTUS effectively decided that corporate rights supersede those of the individual. We see in the Hobby Lobby case that the right to religious freedom neither protected the freedom of individual conscience nor the right to private religious beliefs or acts, but protected the rights of a for-profit corporation to avoid providing what the law required of them regarding otherwise private (reproduction) choices of the individuals that work for them. In the words of Winnifred Sullivan, the Hobby Lobby decision privileged the corporation over the individual (see Sullivan 2020).

The Hobby Lobby case complicates the David and Goliath trope that is common in conversations about religious freedom. The romantic story in which a hero follows their religious conscience in the face of popular, greedy opposition and sticks it to the big guy is hardly the epic moral victory it sounds like when the "person" fighting for religious freedom is a nonreligious, for-profit corporation who refuses to provide basic health care otherwise considered essential for "the little guy." As Finbarr Curtis points out, we assume religious freedom protects "flesh and blood human beings," but this case suggests that the protection is not for flesh and blood human beings but for a corporation.

When we think of religious freedom, we likely are not thinking of the free religious exercise of corporations. We may think about the rights of an owner of a business, like the baker who refused to bake a cake or the florist who refused to provide flowers for gay weddings, but religious freedom is often understood to protect people and a corporation is not generally understood to be a person. The Hobby Lobby case redefined *the who* of religious freedom and extended RFRA and its protections to a corporation. Now, corporations are given religious freedom protections over the rights of the individuals who work for them. As Kathryn Lofton provocatively suggests, this understanding of *the who* of religious freedom makes it "better to be a corporation than a human being" (see Lofton 2017).

Conclusion

The phrase "religious freedom" is so common that we tend to take it for granted and assume we know what it means. What we suggest, though, is that when we ask questions about *what* is protected as religion by the First Amendment and *who* gets to access that protection, we see that religious freedom is not a static, clear, or stable thing. Instead, it is an everchanging set of court decisions and legislation that defines and redefines *the who* and *the what* of religious freedom in an ongoing process. As we saw in *Church of the Lukumi Babalu Aye v. City of Hialeah* (1993), religious freedom did not protect actions like the Free Exercise Clause of the First Amendment would suggest until SCOTUS ruled that it did. *Burwell v. Hobby Lobby Stores, Inc.* (2014) showed us that religious freedom is less about protecting the individual and more about protecting corporate rights. Unlike the popular cliché, religious freedom is not about guaranteeing the rights of individuals who claim something they do (or do not do) is religious. Rather, religious freedom is a set of court decisions and legislation making and remaking the category "religion" in ways that, upon closer examination, might surprise us.

3

"All Religions Are against LGBTQ Rights"

James Crossley

To help us understand the cliché that "All religions are against LGBTQ rights," we might begin with some of its most prominent late twentieth- and early twenty-first-century advocates who see religion as inevitably bigoted and thus inevitably hostile toward LGBTQ rights. At the turn of the millennium, the popular cultural phenomenon known as "New Atheism" was associated with journalists and public intellectuals (notably, Richard Dawkins, Sam Harris, Christopher Hitchens, and Daniel Dennett) who, through bestselling books, media appearances, and newspaper articles, popularized old arguments about religion(s) as irrational and the root cause of much of the violence, bigotry, and intolerance in the world (for discussion, see, e.g., Beattie 2007; Eagleton 2009; McAnulla, Kettell, and Schulzke 2018). Such publications and prominent public debates came to the fore after 9/11, the blame for which was likewise laid at the door of the irrational, intolerant, and destructive power of "religion" (e.g., Dawkins 2001). This has typically meant that Islam was understood as the worst offender (see, e.g., Harris 2004: 105–52), with some Asian religious traditions being romanticized as more tolerant than Christianity, Judaism, and Islam. Nevertheless, a corollary of this claim was a warning that left unchecked all religions similarly lead to violence, bigotry, and intolerance, and potentially more 9/11s. As the novelist and relentless critic of Islam Martin Amis put it, "Since it is no longer permissible to disparage any single faith or creed, let us start disparaging all of them. . . a religion is a belief system with no basis in reality whatever. Religious belief is without reason and without dignity, and its record is near-universally dreadful" (Amis 2002).

So, what has such hostility toward Islam and religion got to do with questions of gender and sexuality? In New Atheist circles, ranking high among the list of intolerances and bigotries supposedly intertwined with religion, and a key reason why religion should therefore be rejected, were issues involving sexuality and gender, and homosexuality, more specifically. In a chapter on "What's Wrong with Religion?" in his bestselling book *The God Delusion*, Dawkins has a section on "Faith and Homosexuality" (Dawkins 2006: 289–91). His interconnected assumptions about what religion entails are important for understanding his argument on homosexuality and further indicative of some of the wider debates we will analyze later. In this context, Dawkins focused primarily on what he called "absolutist" and "fundamentalist" religion and its especially harsh attitudes toward homosexuality where the curtailment of rights is understood in the strong sense (e.g., punishment by death, punishment by mutilation, and divine punishment by AIDS) as well as a lack of legal representation. In contrast to scientific and evidence-based thinking, such "fundamentalists" are people who "know they are right because they have read the truth in a holy book and they know, in advance, that nothing will budge them from their belief." Dawkins argues that this "absolutism" rules "the minds of a great number of people in the world today," most dangerously so "in the Muslim world and in the incipient American theocracy" (Dawkins 2006: 282).

For Dawkins and others, hostility to LGBTQ-related issues is an important and recurring indication of the problem with religion generally across different social and geographical contexts. For instance, as examples of the often-deadly hostility toward homosexuality, Dawkins turned to the Taliban and a range of conservative American preachers as well as a typical reference to relatively recent British history designed to shock an assumed liberal British audience about just how close to home some of these intolerant beliefs are. Dawkins' definition of "fundamentalist religion" blends into his wider ideas about religion per se and help explain why he is "hostile to religion" (Dawkins 2006: 286). The lethal absolutism revealed in the examples of hostility toward homosexuality "nearly always," Dawkins argues, derives from "strong religious faith," and it constitutes "a major reason for suggesting that religion can be a force for evil in the world" (Dawkins 2006: 289). For Dawkins, then, "non-fundamentalist" and "sensible" religion may not seem to be extremism, but it is still connected to its more notorious counterpart in that it makes "the world safe for fundamentalism by teaching children, from their earliest years, that unquestioning faith is a virtue," concluding that "attitudes to homosexuality reveal much about the sort of morality that is inspired by religious faith" (Dawkins 2006: 286, 291).

The Problem of Definitions: LGBTQ

As Dawkins' examples show, there are certainly plenty of instances of what would commonly be understood as religious justifications for homophobia. Outside Islam, the most prominent example of a homophobic religious commandment highlighted by New Atheists (and discussed far beyond) involves the apparent prohibition of male homoeroticism in Judaism and Christianity and the biblical text, Lev. 18:22: "You shall not lie with a male as one lies with a female; it is an abomination." Is Lev. 18:22 a homophobic commandment? It has certainly been interpreted that way and it is not difficult to see why. But things are still not straightforward. I deliberately used the term "homoeroticism" in relation to my description of the text because Leviticus appears to denote a sexual act without necessarily including what has conventionally been understood as a key part of defining homosexuality: "sexual orientation." Indeed, it is a common interpretation in confessional circles to claim that Lev. 18:22 does not condemn a man having sexual feelings for other men but rather condemns the sexual action itself. This hardly constitutes a "pro-gay" reading, of course, but it does complicate what is meant by "homosexuality" in relation to ideas about religious hostility.

Looking closer at the assumptions driving conventional definitions, then, starts to complicate the cliché of our title. One major problem in trying to understand what a text like Lev. 18:22 is prohibiting is that the now familiar categories "homosexual" and "heterosexual" emerge from nineteenth-century European constructions. We can see this in the history of translations of the biblical text 1 Cor. 6:9-10: "Fornicators, idolaters, adulterers, *malakoi*, *arsenokoitai*, thieves, the greedy, drunkards, revilers, robbers—none of these will inherit the kingdom of God." I have left the Greek transliterated but *malakoi* is related to ideas of "soft" and "effeminate," while *arsenokoitai* seems to concern lying down with men. Precisely how we should translate these terms into idiomatic English is for another time; for now, we can note how translations have changed over time. Modern translations will vary but, even with some emphasis on the sexual act, there is a clear implication of sexual orientation in the common use of the word "homosexuality" to translate these words, for example, "men who practice homosexuality" (English Standard Version), "practising homosexuals of whichever sort" (Tom Wright's *New Testament for Everyone*), and "homosexual perverts" (Good News Bible). When we compare this with major premodern translations from the late fourteenth century to the early seventeenth century, there is no obvious word available for a sexual orientation and the focus is on literal translation of ideas relating to manliness and the sexual act itself, for example, "neither lechers against kind, they that do lechery with men" (Wycliffe Bible, English updated), "nether weaklinges nether abusars of them selves with the mankynde" (Tyndale New Testament), "nor effeminate, nor abusers of themselves with mankind" (King James Bible), "nor wantons, nor buggerers" (Geneva Bible), "nor the effeminate, nor the liers with mankind" (Douay-Rheims Bible).

Consequently, the idea of "homosexuality" (or "gay," "lesbian," and "bisexual") as a recognizable orientation and romantic or sexual attraction does not necessarily work as a straightforward comparative description across time and place—and this is likewise a problem for analyzing ancient texts like Leviticus or 1 Corinthians. Indeed, the debate continues as to whether the *concept* of "homosexuality" as we know it is common across time and place even if the corresponding words do not necessarily exist. In critical discussions of the history of sexuality, this has raised a range of questions which have only further complicated popular definitions (the classic debates include, e.g., Foucault 1979, 1985, 1986; Boswell 1980; Halperin 1990, 2002). Are sexuality and sexual deviance modern Western constructs that came to be understood independently, for instance, of class or gender? Does a particular type of sexual activity reveal a person's deep-rooted or inherent sexuality? The debates over when, how, and why such questions emerged in human (and especially Western) history continues, but for all the disagreements and qualifications made in these discussions, a basic point emerges: categorizing sex, sexual activity, homoeroticism, sexuality, sexual deviancy, and so on is dependent on, and will vary according to, historical and cultural contexts.

Already, then, we can see that the problem of establishing whether "religion" (assuming a stable definition of that term for the moment) is invariably hostile toward homosexuality across time and place has already become more difficult and complicated, requiring different definitional questions to ask of our data and precise historical and cultural knowledge of any number of societies. Debates likewise continue over whether homoeroticism (for instance) and identities associated with gender and sexuality are too connected with particular times and places that they can usefully map onto our terminology. Moreover, contemporary debates influenced by queer theory now typically involve navigating, challenging, complicating, or collapsing the binary categories of "gay" and "straight," "female" and "male," "man" and "woman," and "masculine" and "feminine," by foregrounding a range of identifications, some of which may be different to those assigned at birth. This has also involved ideas of gender and sexuality as performative, changing from context to context, or as part of self-identity (classic discussion includes, e.g., Butler 1990; Sedgwick 1990).

These increasingly diverse understandings of gender and sexuality in turn reflect the expansion of the label LGB (Lesbian, Gay, Bisexual) beyond apparent sexual orientation to variations on LGBTQ (Lesbian, Gay, Bisexual, Transgender, Queer/Questioning). Irrespective of whether we can use categories like "homosexuality" or "queer" to describe contexts where no comparable word exists, it is clear enough that labeling as well as defining gender and sexuality is historically and culturally conditioned, constantly accumulating or dropping assumptions. But there are further complications, and already I have started using "gender" and "sexuality" alongside each other. When Dawkins and his fellow New Atheists of the 2000s utilized an established cliché, they too were also of their time where LGB rights and acceptance had become increasingly embedded in liberal societies. With the benefit of hindsight, there is another way we can now see Dawkins as of his time and how a given cliché is at the mercy of historical and social change. Dawkins used the term "homosexual" rather than the now conventional term (or variants) used in the title of this essay: "LGBTQ." Today, LGBTQ (or variants) is not only a more conventional label but one which obviously differs in use from a label "homosexuality" alone. In particular, the "T" has become central to some of the most high-profile Western cultural debates in the past decade and was not a central part of public debates when Dawkins published *The God Delusion* in 2006.

Certainly, it is obvious enough that the cliché that religions are against LGBTQ rights is related to the cliché that religions are against LGB rights. But the T and the Q are not straightforwardly related to the L, G, or B. A common understanding of "transgender" or "trans" is that the term refers to identification of gender identity, which may at times or always be understood as different to the sex a person was assigned at birth and can be related to other terms such as "nonbinary" and "genderqueer," among others. In and of themselves, the terms do not give any indication of sexual preference, or indeed if a trans person has any sexual interests at all. If the contemporary American-led culture wars tell us anything, it is that there are Christians who oppose people's claim to gender self-identity if it differs from the sex assigned at birth who are likewise opposed to homoerotic relations or homosexuality in general. These people would thus seem to support the idea that religion is against LGBTQ, even if they explained their opposition to homosexuality, homoeroticism, and gender self-identity with reference to different justifications and different biblical texts.

But to complicate matters further, self-identification and the T in LGBTQ has caused problems for Dawkins himself. For Dawkins' ideal world freed from religious bigotry, a world based on evidence and science, gender self-identification has been a complicating issue. For instance, Dawkins tweeted:

Is trans woman a woman? Purely semantic. If you define by chromosomes, no. If by self-identification, yes. I call her "she" out of courtesy. (@RichardDawkins, October 26, 2015)

In 2015, Rachel Dolezal, a white chapter president of NAACP, was vilified for identifying as Black. Some men choose to identify as women, and some women choose to identify as men. You will be vilified if you deny that they literally are what they identify as. Discuss. (@RichardDawkins, April 10, 2021)

In his clarification, Dawkins continued to construct his position in relation to rationality and distance himself from any implied right-wing Christian connotations:

I do not intend to disparage trans people. I see that my academic "Discuss" question has been misconstrued as such and I deplore this. It was also not my intent to ally in any way with Republican bigots in US now exploiting this issue. (@RichardDawkins, April 12, 2021)

This is a good indication of how public debates over sexuality and gender have moved on since 2006 as once obvious ideological allies are now rejecting Dawkins' position. The American Humanist Association withdrew its 1996 Humanist of the Year award from Dawkins and constructed Dawkins' behavior if not as "religious," then at least as the opposite of that expected of a humanist:

Richard Dawkins has over the past several years accumulated a history of making statements that use the guise of scientific discourse to demean marginalized groups, an approach antithetical to humanist values. His latest statement implies that the identities of transgender individuals are fraudulent, while also simultaneously attacking Black identity as one that can be assumed when convenient. His subsequent attempts at clarification are inadequate and convey neither sensitivity nor sincerity. (American Humanist Association 2021)

Has Dawkins' emphasis on science and humanism begun to lead him toward downgrading trans people? That could be one reading of Dawkins' first tweet, but it is one clearly challenged by the American Humanist Association. For the American Humanist Association, the opposite seems to be the case: being a good humanist and scientist is not compatible with such questioning of trans identity. But what this debate obviously reveals is that a person can take any number of positions on gender and sexuality and still claim to be a scientist or humanist, even if the idealized meanings of such labels are contested among participants in the debate. And if we can complicate definitions of what a scientist and humanist are expected to believe, then we can do the same for what religious people are expected to believe.

The Problem of Definitions: Religion

The cliché that all religions are against LGBTQ in all its diversity no doubt works with another cliché, namely that the representatives of such religions might be (say) a Trump-supporting pastor or a conservative Islamic cleric. But note how these definitions of the religious people require explanations like "Trump-supporting" and "conservative cleric." Yet, like scientists and humanists, there are people claiming to be religious who take opposing views, openly promoting the compatibility between their understanding of religion or a religious tradition and LGBTQ in all its diversity or some parts of L, G, B, T, or Q. Today, there is a common liberal tradition employed by some Christians and Jews of reading Lev. 18:22 not against male homoeroticism or homosexuality per se but against some other sexual practice (e.g., male prostitution in temples and rape), thereby ensuring the Bible is not opposed to male homoeroticism at least. There are likewise common readings made by Christians and Jews claiming that Lev, 18:22 might be homophobic (for instance) but that the text is outdated, anachronistic, or overridden by more important tolerant sentiments in the Bible such as love (see the following discussion).

Even if somewhat blurry in its precise definitions of LGBT, a visually striking use of biblical interpretation is the Queen James Bible (QJB). Based on the King James Bible, the QJB has a rainbow-colored cross on its front cover and edited to "prevent homophobic misinterpretation" by discrediting an earlier translation of the Bible: "homosexuality was first mentioned in the Bible in 1946, in the Revised Standard Version." The advertising places the QJB in opposition to "Anti-LGBT Bible interpretations," where the Bible is interpreted "to mean homosexuality is a sin." It is also claimed that King James himself "was a well-known bisexual" who married women but "his many gay relationships were so well-known that. . . he was known as 'Queen James.'" The QJB is a Bible expected to be used in what might be understood as religious settings, "for ceremony, study, sermon, gift-giving, or simply to put on display in the home or Church" (Queen James Bible 2012). Today, there is a thriving theological tradition of sexuality, gender, transgender, and intersex studies, which has become known part of (for instance) some Anglican and Episcopal churches (e.g., among many, Beardsley and O'Brien, no date; 2016). The Church of the Ascension at Blackheath, London, put it simply in its short statement of belief the sentence, "We are fully supportive of human rights in this church and are active in campaigning for changes in attitudes towards LGBT+ people in the wider church" (Church of the Ascension, no date).

While such declarations of LGBTQ support are obviously of our time, constructions of gender fluidity and speculations beyond gender binaries in religious traditions are not necessarily new. In rabbinic Judaism, there are passages which blur bodies and ideas of "male" and "female," with men miraculously growing breasts and lactating, even if they do not always escape ideas of male dominance and normative expectations for men (Kessler 2007: 394–6). A related point can be made about the construction of sexuality. In their study of premodern Jains, Leonard Zwilling and Michael Sweet (1996) write of the modern-sounding constructions of gender and sexuality in "Jain religious literature." They locate some of their analysis on the context of pan-Indian "acceptance of a third sex," speculations about what the nature of the third sex might be in relation to a man or a woman, and the development of a "full-fledged conception of sexuality. . . a sexuality that is often, but not invariably, linked to gender nonconformity and biological sex." They further note descriptions of "organizational expedience in accepting sexually nonnormative individuals into the order if they were not too effeminate, followed the rules, and/or had some valued skill" (Zwilling and Sweet 1996: 361–2, 383). In this latter instance, it should be obvious that I stray from my limited knowledge rooted in the Anglophone world and their most prominent religious traditions (a limitation I share with Dawkins), but equally it is the case that there is a wide-ranging discussion across the diverse areas of Asian studies and Asian religious studies on such issues (e.g., recently, among many more, Hinchy 2022). Despite my limitations, then, the principle is the same: experts in a range of religious traditions and cultural contexts will be able to cite many more examples from across time and place to show that the cliché that religion is against LGBTQ constantly breaks down. This is because of simple point: there are people and texts associated with religious traditions taking the exact opposite line, having different assumptions of sexuality and gender to modern Western ones, or have traditions which engage with and complicate expectations of physiology, gender, and sexuality.

Our definition of "religion" is, then, as malleable and context dependent as the language of sexuality and gender. This can be highlighted by again looking at these ideas with reference to "religion" and "religions" more generally beyond the Anglophone world. With reference to a sociological study of data about values and attitudes in fifty-five countries in the period 2010–14 by Dirk-Jan Janssen and Peer Scheepers. They claimed that a rejection of homosexuality was associated with all aspects of "religiosity," which they defined as, for instance, religious institutions and attendance, beliefs, experiences, knowledge, and pervasiveness in everyday lives. And to their surprise, their results showed that Hindus were more likely still to reject homosexuality than Muslims (Janssen and Scheepers 2018). A problem facing these sorts of studies, yet again, is one of definition. Anyone starting the critical study of religion will soon be confronted by how many contested scholarly attempts at defining "religion" there are and by a debate similar to the definition of "homosexuality": does the concept "religion" exist if there is no such equivalent word in a given society? And, likewise, if we change the definition, then the results even of a learned sociological paper will likely change too. What if those behaviors deemed "religious" were justifications for attitudes which are entangled with a range of other cultural and historic factors that are not so easily isolated from one another? What if definitions of "religion" could not do justice to the behaviors and attitudes of billions of people over vast geographical areas with hugely diverse histories?

Certainly, the kind of sociological study carried out by Janssen and Scheepers is hardly without its merits and can give us insights on their own terms, but understandings of "religion" and "religiosity" and comparable terms have changed and will change over time and in different places. We might, then, approach our data on religion and LGBTQ in a manner that pays attention to such historical and cultural differences and change. Put another way, we can also analyze evidence, which does *not* support the cliché about religions opposing LGBTQ rights, such as presented in the work carried out by the LGBTQ+ charity Stonewall on people who identify as (for instance) LGBT, lesbian, gay, or genderqueer and (for instance) Muslim, Christian, Jewish, or Hindu (O'Connor and Cohen 2015; Gander 2017). This is not to say who is and who is not a "true" believer or who has and has not interpreted the sacred texts better. Nor is this to downplay the historic difficulties LGBTQ people have faced in a variety of settings associated with religions. Instead, the analyst of religion can also ask questions about how and why religion or a given religion is being used to authorize or deny identities based on sexuality and gender and provide various historical and cultural explanations for this.

Making Different Clichés

Retreating to my comfort zone, but nonetheless to make a point with broader applicability, let us take the example of English political discourse where public definitions or assumptions about religion have changed as social attitudes toward LGBTQ people have changed. Indeed, the twenty-first century has seen a striking reversal in the presentation of religion and homosexuality, from once being deemed incompatible to both categories now being integral to one another (for a summary of religion in recent English political history, see Crossley 2018, 10–29). Where Dawkins sees religion and the Bible fostering irrationality, bigotry, and intolerance, English politicians will now typically assume that religion and the Bible, understood correctly, foster tolerance, inclusion, and equal rights. In the discussion of the "Marriage (Same Sex Couples)" Bill in 2013 (which led to the introduction of "same-sex marriage" in England and Wales), whenever Jesus and the Bible were invoked in the parliamentary debate, they were used in support of the Bill, such as in the following statements by three different politicians:

I as a Christian have no worries about voting for this Bill. What greater example of the equalities agenda could there be than Jesus Christ himself?

The Jesus I know was born a refugee, illegitimate, with a death warrant on his name, and in a barn among animals. He would stand up for minorities. That is why it is right for those of religious conviction to vote for this Bill. . . those on the extremes of our faith have poisoned what is an important debate with references to polygamy and bestiality.

The primary commandment is to love the Lord my God with all my heart, soul, mind and strength. I have been reminded by one ordained constituent that that should be used as a way of defining the second great commandment, which is to treat my neighbour as myself. Essentially, we are asking whether we can remove the barriers that stop same-sex couples enjoying the commitment—the "at one" meaning—of marriage. That is what the Bill comes down to. It does not redefine marriage; it just takes away barriers. (Hansard 2013)

There was some opposition on religious grounds, but it was muted, and the three examples discussed in the chapter represent what has become a dominant understanding of religion in English political discourse in the twenty-first century. The country has become increasingly tolerant of LGB (at least) over the past forty years, with those identifying with a particular Christian tradition following the lead of those who do not identify with any religious tradition, and across a range of questions (e.g., sexual relations, marriage, and adoption) (see Clements 2015, 2017). Consequently, so too has the religion, Jesus, Christianity, and Bible of mainstream English politicians changed to reflect this. Once again, we see how social and historical change clearly dictates what becomes the next cliché.

Nevertheless, one of the problems such understandings of religion and the Bible faces is a well-known history of interpretation, which is anything but supportive of LGBTQ rights. To deal with this issue, interpreters, such as the politicians cited previously, present their arguments as the normative center (e.g., "It does not redefine marriage" and "What greater example of the equalities agenda") and make the socially illiberal arguments the problem (e.g., "those on the extremes of our faith"). The reference to Jesus is important; there is a long history of understanding Jesus as representing kindly, liberal, radical, or even socialist values over against illiberal or oppressive ones, and today he is regularly invoked in liberal discourses as someone who never condemned homosexuality and (thus) nor should Christians or anyone who follows or respects him (see the following).

Consequently, what we also find in such discourses is a tension between the purer or progressive religion and sacred texts (on the one hand) and "false" or "distorting" interpretations of religion and the sacred texts (on the other) (cf. also Dawkins 2006: 235–62). In mainstream English political discourse, homophobic interpretations of sacred texts are typically understood as deviations from a purer tolerant origin or the supposed core of religion. To take a typical example, the politician Angela Eagle criticized an opposing politician, Tim Farron, who was understood to believe sexual intercourse between men was a sin by claiming he was "an *evangelical* Christian who believes in the *literal* truth of the bible" at a time of "a huge revival of *fundamentalist* religious belief" yet he "just doesn't want to talk about it a lot because he knows how much it will embarrass his own party" (Hattenstone 2015, my italics). The language here is important, and the qualifications "literal," "fundamentalist," and "evangelical" were being used not as an attack on Christianity, the Bible, or religion but as an attack on the perceived distortion or an excessive misinterpretation of a purer Christianity, Bible, and religion compatible with LGB (at least) rights.

This approach also means that politicians can prioritize certain parts of the Bible or contextualize any problematic parts as belonging to a distant irrelevant history, particularly in the case of the recurring problem of Lev. 18:22. In an interview with the magazine, *Attitude*, the former prime minister of the UK, Tony Blair, recommended re-reading Leviticus in a way that would remove its illiberal sting (and note the typical negative qualification "literal"):

> when people quote the passages in Leviticus condemning homosexuality, I say to them—if you read the whole of the Old Testament and took everything that was there in a literal way, as being what God and religion is about, you'd have some pretty tough policies across the whole of the piece . . . and you've got the Old Testament kings with hordes of concubines, and so on. There's no way that you could take all of that and say, we in the 21st century should behave in that way. (Hari 2009)

For Blair, the Bible and Christianity—properly understood—are comparable to all other sacred texts and religions generally and the correct understanding of all religions is controlled by an understanding that the essence of religion is tolerance, liberalism, and democracy (Crossley 2016: 210–41). Thus, Blair can prioritize religious founding figures at the origins of a religion because here we see the "true" religious impulse that drove them to change the world:

> And actually, what people often forget about, for example, Jesus or, indeed, the Prophet Mohammed, is that their whole raison d'être was to change

the way that people thought traditionally. Christianity was very much about saying, no, "an eye for an eye, a tooth for a tooth" is not the right way to behave. And the Koran was, of course, an extraordinary, progressive—revolutionarily progressive—document for its time. That's why many of the old pagan practices that the Prophet was keen to wean people away from were dispensed with. (Hari 2009)

The argument here is that Jesus and Mohammed challenged the intolerances of their day and founded progressive religions, the supposed true meanings of which have sometimes been obscured by later intolerant believers. For Blair, this progressive impulse can get lost over time and he now puts his hope in "people," the communal wisdom of the congregation, and a younger generation who reject official or traditional views of homosexuality. As he put it in the interview:

what is interesting is that if you went into any Catholic Church, particularly a well-attended one, on any Sunday here and did a poll of the congregation, you'd be surprised at how liberal-minded people were. . . . On many issues, I think the leaders of the Church and the Church will be in complete agreement. But I think on some of these issues, if you went and asked the congregation, I think you'd find that their faith is not to be found in those types of entrenched attitudes. If you asked "what makes you religious?" and "what does your faith mean to you?" they would immediately go into compassion, solidarity, relieving suffering. I would be really surprised if they went to "actually, it's to do with believing homosexuality is wrong" or "it's to do with believing this part of the ritual or doctrine should be done in this particular way." (Hari 2009)

The argument here is that younger generations with liberal values are the legitimate inheritors of the progressive impulse of religion by their practical focus on what "really matters" and not being interested in topics that are potentially illiberal, such as criticizing homosexuality. It is striking what "faith" means here and how it is vague enough to be necessarily compatible with equally vague liberal democratic values: compassion, solidarity, and relieving suffering. It is not about anything deemed too culturally weird for public presentations of religion (e.g., whether the specifics of "ritual and doctrine" or condemning homosexuality). Again, then: once the definition is changed, the clichés about religion change accordingly.

In this respect, Blair's understanding of homosexuality and religion reflects the dominant one in English political discourse today to the point that it has become a major cliché in its own right. To show this, we can look further at the case of Tim Farron (for details, see Crossley 2018: 56–63). Farron was the leader of the Liberal Democratic Party between 2015 and 2017 and was associated with Christian groups who believed "homosexual sex" was a sin (to use the phrase from interviews with Farron). This emphasis on "homosexual sex" was deliberate: it was picking up on the interpretation of Lev. 18:22, which claims it is the sexual action rather than sexual orientation that is being condemned. While it was widely assumed that Farron did indeed believe homosexual sex was a sin, he did not publicly admit it because it would signal the end of his career as a leader of a major political party. To avoid the issue, Farron made the classic liberal distinction between his *personal* Christian morality and his *public* political liberalism, which tolerates other groups and individuals, irrespective of whether they are personally agreeable (notably, Farron stressed his record of supporting LGBTQ legal rights, including emphasizing transgender rights). To get around difficult questions in interviews, he made general theological statements that all people are sinners and even tried to make the move typical of mainstream politicians, namely stressing a more "liberal" part of the Bible over a more "illiberal" part. When the interviewer Cathy Newman raised the question of the seemingly illiberal Lev. 18:22, Farron responded by pointing to Jesus instead and a passage which would sit more easily with contemporary liberalism: Matt. 7:3 ("You don't pick out the speck of sawdust in your brother's eye when there is a plank in your own"; Farron's paraphrase) (Channel 4 2015). Unlike Blair and others, Farron faced the problem that he was still associated with the idea that homosexual sex is sinful and the common assumption in mainstream political discourse that that being personally and secretively critical of homosexual sex was not an option for a leader of a main political party. Farron's views came under greater scrutiny when a General Election was called in 2017 and he eventually claimed that homosexual sex was *not* a sin, which did not work for him as he was understood to be a hypocrite, including by colleagues from within his own party, and this issue effectively led to his resignation.

What the example of Farron shows is just how embedded the idea that a "true" understanding of religion, Christian, Christianity, and the Bible (to which we can include religions like Islam) in mainstream English political discourse must not only support LGBTQ (or at least LGB) rights but must also mean that leading politicians should be supportive in both private and public. We have now emphatically arrived at the reverse stereotype of the one in the title: all religions are *for* LGBTQ (or at least LGB) rights! Strikingly, after Farron quit as leader and was away from frontbench politics, he implicitly admitted what most suspected and then staked a claim to the "true" meaning of Christianity and the Bible. He spoke about how he was "torn between living as a faithful Christian and serving as a political leader" and the tension involved in remaining "faithful to Christ while leading a political party in the current environment." However, he concluded that being a leader of "a progressive liberal party in 2017" and "a committed Christian" who wanted "to hold faithful to the Bible's teaching" was "impossible" (BBC 2017; cf. Farron 2017). What this logic implies is that people who claim to be Christian and think homosexual sex is not a sin are *unfaithful* to the Bible and Christ and ultimately not truly Christian. However, that Farron could still present these views in the mainstream media is important. The media provides a platform where the old cliché still remains (either in acceptance or opposition)—but remains in competition with the emerging cliché that being religious means accepting LGB(TQ) people and supporting LGB(TQ) rights.

A Clash of Clichés

When the comedian and actor Russell Brand published his book *Revolution* on politics and the progressive power of meditation and "true" religion (Brand 2014), it was met with ridicule in the media. While most reviews avoided or denied Brand's embrace of Christianity and preferred to mock his interest in various "Eastern" religions, one openly atheist reviewer (Nick Cohen) provided a Dawkins-style critique, notably on the issue of religion and homosexuality:

> Anyone who claims that Jesus, Allah, Krishna or the fountainhead of any other religion endorses homophobia instead of the "union of all mankind" is "on a massive blag" [i.e., to get or achieve something by deceitful means], he [Brand] says. Brand has to ignore Leviticus's edict that the punishment for men who sleep with other men is death, St Paul's hysterics about lesbianism and the hadiths that have Muhammad saying that the punishment for sodomy is death by stoning. In other words, he has to ignore several millennia of real and continuing religious repression, so he can make his spiritualism sound emancipatory rather than cranky. (Cohen 2014)

According to Cohen, Brand's claim that religious founders and sacred texts are progressive is ludicrous and tried to undermine Brand by showing that these sacred texts are instead violently nonprogressive on the issue of homoeroticism. In doing so, Cohen reversed the cliché that all religions are tolerant at heart but have been distorted by later intolerant interpreters by instead arguing that religions are intolerant at heart and have been distorted by later tolerant interpreters.

However, Cohen did not always represent Brand fairly because Brand did not ignore the biblical texts. Brand argued in *Revolution* that Jesus did *not* talk about homosexuality but did talk about love (another popular cliché connected with religion, we might add), and Brand included an extended joke about the

Ten Commandments where "God would prefer you to have gay sex than covet your neighbour's oxen" (Brand 2014: 66–7). Against Cohen, Brand *did* discuss the notorious Leviticus passage and made the familiar move that Leviticus' prohibition of a man lying with a man is an anomaly and not a priority for God because it is not mentioned in the Ten Commandments (Brand 2014: 66–7). My point here is not, of course, to referee the rights and wrongs of the respective interpretations but to show that the respective interpretations and clichés are currently in competition with one another, at least in the Anglophone media and public debate.

In terms of clashing stereotypes, this is where the transgender, queer, and related classifications involved in LGBTQ+ definitions are now prominent. In some ways, the debate is familiar. When the singer Demi Lovato revealed their preferred pronouns were "they/them," Jenna Ellis, who had worked on Donald Trump's legal team, tweeted:

> Interesting that the only time in scripture an individual was referred to in plural "they/their/we" pronouns is in Matthew 5:9. Jesus asked a demon-possessed man his name, and he replied, "My name is Legion, for we are many." (@JennaEllisEsq, May 24, 2021)

No doubt, the American-led culture wars will see plenty more transphobic statements in the foreseeable future because the cliché about religions being against LGBTQ rights and very validity of the LGBTQ individual is not without examples. But the alternative cliché is likewise common and, while transgender and queer issues have high-profile irreligious critics like Dawkins, it is a familiar stereotype inherited from the previous decades of LGB advocacy. For instance, Megan Rohrer—who became the first transgender Christian bishop in America after being elected by the Evangelical Lutheran Church in 2021—claimed, "Lutherans have once again declared that transgender people are beautiful children of God." Rohrer was likewise aware of the power of the competing claims and how this is a clash of ideologies, adding, "We need to all be as loud and as angry as the people who want to declare that there are types of people that God can't love" (O'Donnell 2021). Similarly, the Presbyterian pastor Mac Schafer, father of the transgender model and actress Hunter Schafer, has argued in ways familiar from debates we have seen about LGB:

> LGBTQ folks are beautifully and wonderfully made by God and are an essential part of the human community. Everything we know about the ministry of Jesus tells us to work for the liberation, freedom and the full humanity of all people. As people of faith we are always working to come down on the side of compassion, and justice, because that's what Christ modeled so boldly in his ministry. (Schafer 2021)

A key theme linking the LGB with the TQ is that the language of religion is normalized as the agreeable, familiar. In addition, the language of tolerance, love, decency, democracy, etc. is authoritative. In American public discourse, it is not overly dramatic to claim that the clash of stereotypes over LGBTQ rights and religion is a clash over the very meaning and direction of American democracy itself. Just as Trump has his high-profile anti-LGBTQ support, it was little surprise that Joe Biden's inaugural prayer service was openly inclusive of LGBTQ participants (Wakefield 2021), which can be seen as feeding into including progressive myths of national uniqueness (cf. Puar 2007).

Concluding Remarks

"All religions are against LGBTQ rights" may be a factually problematic cliché, but it is not difficult to see why it is used. Countless stories of the (sometimes life-threatening) struggles of LGBTQ people across religious traditions and cultural contexts exist. These stories are no surprise, and we can expect more. Whenever there is a natural disaster, we can likewise expect some high-profile religious representative claiming it is divine punishment for acceptance of LGBTQ rights, or the like. But, in Anglophone discourses at least, gathering momentum is an alternative cliché based on the assumption that religion is about peace, love, tolerance, democracy, and so on, namely that LGBTQ rights are a logical extension of this assumption. Of course, if we revisit this topic in (say) America twenty years from now, with changing demographics and shifting political concerns, we may well see different assumptions emerge, or certain ones start to dominate. For now, for or against LGBTQ rights, for or against religion, such competing clichés all assume the authoritative power of religion. This is why, as students and scholars of religion, we should take a critical approach not just to popular uses of such clichés but their application in the critical study of religion itself. Definitions of and assumptions about religion and specific religions carry a history of competing ideological claims, and our choice of definitions will dictate our use of data. If there is anything close to certainty in all this, it is that the choice of how religion is defined will likewise dictate its relationship to one of the most prominent topics in contemporary Anglophone understandings of religion: LGBTQ rights. While I have largely limited myself to Anglophone examples, not least because of the prominence of such a cliché in my own cultural contexts, it should be stressed that the principles of understanding how discourses on sexuality, gender, and religion itself are dependent on, and change in, historical and cultural contexts apply to the study of religion generally and any given religions specially. If one generalization ought to remain it is that the counterexamples to any cliché about religion will constantly be found in religious traditions across time and place.

4

"Spirituality Is about Spirituality"

Brad Stoddard and Craig Martin

In 2017, the Pew Research Center found that over "a quarter of U.S. adults (27%) now say they think of themselves as spiritual but not religious" (SBNR; Lipka and Gecewicz). This figure is 8 percentage points higher than a similar study just five years earlier, suggesting that people who identify as SBNR is not only increasing but increasing rapidly. People who identify as SBNR are almost equally split between women and men; they are found in various races and ethnicities, and they include members of both major political parties. Academic research on people who identify as SBNR repeatedly demonstrates that these people are skeptical of institutionalized religion, they question dominant ideas about god(s), and they rarely or never attend formal religious services. Their aversion toward dominant forms of religiosity might suggest they fit the stereotype of secular atheists who at all costs avoid anything and everything related to religion. By embracing the label of "spiritual," however, they suggest that they perhaps believe in, practice, and observe something best described as religion adjacent; that is, "something" related to religion but worthy of a distinct title.

This "something," however, is subject to dispute and disagreement. A quick search of #spiritual or #spirituality on TikTok reveals that spirituality references a rather wide range of activities and practices including massages, reading, walking in nature, reading tarot cards, finding "god within," walking one's dog, practicing "presentism," finding beauty in everything, opening yourself to the universe, mastering negative thoughts, meditating, collecting crystals, taking a bath, applying essential oils, placing plants in your house, and even applying makeup and making love. An even deeper search reveals disagreement as self-professed experts on spirituality argue that some of the things on this list aren't spiritual at all. They disagree on what true spirituality actually is and they're quick to criticize each other over what they consider false or even dangerous practices and beliefs.

While many of these people disagree on the contents of spirituality, they agree that spirituality is about spirituality—that is, that there is something truly unique or distinct about spirituality, which makes it in some way fundamentally different from religion, faith, cults, new religious movements, and so on. As evidenced by the cultural repository and curator that is TikTok, the idea that spirituality is about spirituality is in fact the core belief that unites these diverse and otherwise unrelated activities and beliefs. This idea is the focus of this chapter. This chapter argues that the idea that spirituality is about spirituality is itself a cliché. And as evidenced by the Pew study, it's a growing cliché that is primarily popular among the college educated (i.e., the people most likely reading this book). To explore this cliché, this chapter summarizes the history of the idea that spirituality is about spirituality, examines some of the people who created the intellectual framework for the idea, and concludes by highlighting four main problems with the idea.

Spirituality: A Modern Concept

Long before people made distinctions between "spirituality" and "organized religion," people made almost identical distinctions between "religious experience" and "institutional religion"—the way that people talk about spirituality draws from and reproduces a lot of the assumptions from theories of "religious experience." Consequently, to fully understand "spirituality" talk, we need to briefly review "experience" talk.

Although people who oppose "organized religion" may include "Christianity" among what they want to distinguish themselves from, the experience/ institution distinction was created by Christians themselves. Going back to the seventeenth century, Christian philosophers tended to argue primarily about which Christian doctrines or moral rules were the true ones; there was a great deal of disagreement about which Christian dogmas or Christian ethics were right, but very little disagreement about the centrality of "doctrines" and "morals" to the discussion. This all changed when a German theologian named Friedrich Schleiermacher came along and argued that the focus on Christian doctrine and morality fundamentally misunderstood what was important about Christianity.[1] He argued that experiences of God defined Christianity, not beliefs or behaviors. In addition, he said that this was true of all religions. "Religion's essence is . . . intuition and feeling" (1996, 22), and "[t]o have religion means to intuit the universe" (52). To *feel* God was far more important than what we believe about God or what we think God wants us to do.

And, much like those who say they are "spiritual but not religious," the one term "experience" is used to criticize the other things—doctrines, rituals, sacred texts, and so on. For Schleiermacher, "[e]very holy writing is merely a mausoleum of religion, a monument that a great spirit was there that no longer exists" (50). To paraphrase him, what he means here is that books like the Bible are coffins for the spirit of God, which has long since fled; in this case, we should turn away from empty graves and turn toward living spirits.

Although such claims might appeal to those who distinguish spirituality from religion, it is notable that Schleiermacher goes on to rank religions based on whether they are closer to corpses or the real thing. For instance, he makes a number of anti-Semitic remarks along these lines: "Judaism is long since a dead religion, and those who at present still bear its colors are actually sitting and mourning beside the undecaying mummy and weeping over its demise and sad legacy" (114–115). By contrast, he argues that Christianity—despite its flaws—is much closer to God: "The original intuition of Christianity is more glorious, more sublime, more worthy of adult humanity, more deeply penetrating into the spirit of systematic religion, and extending farther over the whole universe" (115). In sum, Schleiermacher makes a distinction between "experiences" of God and cold, dead "doctrine and ritual" in part because it allows him to justify his claim that Christianity is superior to Judaism.

From the time of Schleiermacher to the present, this sort of distinction has been used to rank traditions and present some as superior to others. Rudolph Otto, in *The Idea of the Holy*, argues that true religion is about experience, and authentic religious experiences can never be put into words; written words pale in comparison to the experiences themselves—much as Schleiermacher described sacred texts as mausoleums for corpses with departed spirits. Once he has set up his distinction between experience and other, secondary matters, he goes on to say that Christianity puts into words what cannot be put into words better than any other religion. He then ranks religions according to how well they prioritize experience: he puts Christianity at the top, followed by Judaism, Islam, and so on; and at the bottom, he puts the religions of people like Africans and Native Americans—the religion of "primitive savages" is rudimentary.

For Schleiermacher and Otto, at the end of the day they say that true religion involves experiences of the divine, but they do so in order to say European religions are superior to the ones found in parts of the world where brown people live. While it is unlikely that those who claim to be spiritual but not religious are equally racist, it is clear that they use the language of spirituality to claim a certain sort of spiritual superiority. It took us only minutes of browsing #spirituality hashtags on TikTok to find such claims to superiority. Consider, for instance, a video by @philgoodlife with the hashtags #relationships, #spiritualtiktok, #spirituality, #spiritual, #consciousness, and #inspiration, in which Phil makes the following claims:

> If you happen to be at a higher level of consciousness—as most of you are, by the way; congratulations!—then you have an ability to openly express yourself. There's no shame. You're able to share what's going on in your life. You're able to let someone in, but you're not necessarily attaching onto what it is you are sharing. That's because you don't hold judgment. You have a wider capacity for conversation. The thing is, if you share that information with someone who is at a lower level of consciousness, which is neither good or bad, it just means they have a smaller capacity to be able to hold space for you. Why? Because they hold more fear and judgment. So everything that you share, they're going to project their judgment onto. So they won't even hear you, because everything is about them. They're caught up in the ego. It's not their fault. They just hold a lot of fear and judgment.

While the speaker claims that there is nothing good or bad about this, we suspect that he would think it was bad if we claimed that *he* was at a lower level of consciousness, that *he* was very fearful and judgmental, or that *he* was caught up in his own ego; despite his claim that he's not criticizing people at a "lower level," this is belied by the fact that he calls it a "lower level." In any case, what is remarkable here is the similarity between his claims and those of Schleiermacher and Otto: we need to be "spiritual," but some of us are better at being "spiritual" than others. The language of experience and spirituality seems fundamentally designed to rank people, and those who claim to be spiritual always put themselves on top.

Though many of the roots of contemporary ideas about spirituality lie outside the United States, there is a distinctly American history to these ideas (Peng 2019). In the 1800s, various groups and their leaders collectively questioned and even criticized dominant religiosity in the United States, resulting in what scholars often term religious liberalism. According to scholar Leigh Eric Schmidt, groups like Transcendentalists, Unitarians, progressive Quakers, and Reform Jews (among others) collectively criticized what they often termed traditional religion. They saw themselves as bridges between oppressive pasts led by authoritarian religious institutions and a more liberated future where individuals, no longer stifled by tradition, were free to chart their own paths. As evidenced by people like Walt Whitman, many of these thinkers associated religion with these oppressive pasts and spirituality with liberated individualism.

Whitman emerged in the 1850s as a highly influential American poet. Though rooted in the Transcendalist movement that taught that divinity existed outside religious institutions in all of nature and in humanity itself, Whitman modified these ideas and associated them with the word "spirituality." In *Democratic Vistas* (published in 1871), for example, Whitman wrote that the "the spirituality of religion" could only be realized in the "solitariness of individuality" (quoted from Schmidt 2012, xiii). Schmidt described the significance of this book when he wrote,

> Whitman's *Democratic Vistas* is revealing not only because of the way it exalts "spirituality" and extracts it from "religion," but also because of the string of closely interconnected concepts it brings into alignment with the spiritual: meditation, solitude, mystical ecstasy, ineffability, freedom, aspiration, and individuality, all of which get juxtaposed with ecclesial institutions. The latter, Whitman claimed, "melt away like vapors" when confront with these boundless "soul energies." (Schmidt xiii)

Democratic Vistas is one example of a larger phenomenon where people criticized traditional religion and espoused the virtues of individual-based spirituality. This association of spirituality and individualism became a foundation of the rhetoric of spirituality that exists today.

In addition to writers like Whitman, other factors in the 1800s also contributed to the evolving rhetoric of spirituality. Chief among them was the World's Parliament of Religions. In 1893, the city of Chicago hosted the World's Columbian Exposition. Designed to celebrate the 400th year of Christopher Columbus' "discovery" of the Americas, the organizers of the Exposition expanded the project's scope when they invited people from around the world to celebrate human innovation in various fields including science, technology, agriculture, and religion, among many others. Organizers created various "Parliaments, or extended meetings where leaders from around the world met to discuss specific topics. The World's Parliament of Religions was one such Parliament, where authority figures from major world religions met for the first time where they interacted and learned about each other's religions firsthand.

The World's Parliament of Religions is important to the rhetoric of spirituality because Americans who were already aware of the terms and who contributed to its evolution learned about practices associated with Asian religions like yoga and meditation. Previously, such Asian practices were classified alongside those of "primitive savages" in Africa or North America, but now these practices began to be included in Americans' evolving notions of spirituality. They were associated with large religions, but individuals practiced yoga and meditation, not just for religious reasons but to improve their health as well. The emphasis on individuals and on their desire to improve their lives dovetailed nicely with notions of spirituality, which similarly stressed individualism and human development. The World's Parliament of Religions ended in 1893, but the proverbial seeds were sown. A growing portion of Americans wanted to learn more about Asian religions and their allegedly "spiritual" practices, so they formed "spiritual retreats" to educate themselves on these practices, they wrote articles and books on the topics, and they helped create a cultural movement that linked their ideas and practices to the words "spiritual" and "spirituality."

These associations continued to develop into the 1900s, particularly in the 1960s, when several factors combined to solidify contemporary notions of spirituality. First, the 1965 Immigration Act played an important role because it changed America's immigration laws. Prior to the 1965 Immigration Act, America's immigration laws favored immigrants from Europe. The Immigration Act, however, removed restrictions on immigrants from other parts of the world. People immigrated to the United States from Africa and Asia. They brought with them their languages and cultures, and also their religions. They found in the United States the growing counterculture movement, where young Americans dubbing themselves "hippies" were already rejecting what they considered traditional American values and religion. Like the religious liberals of the 1800s, these younger Americans believed traditional American values and religion were oppressive or stifling, and they worked to create a future free from these traditions. They adopted parts of Asian religions and associated these practices, first, with their respect for individual expression and development, and second, with the words "spiritual" and "spirituality." In hindsight, they solidified the roots of contemporary notions of spirituality.

As hippies and other countercultural youth matured, to various degrees they either abandoned some of their more revolutionary ideals or chose to ignore them as they integrated into the mainstream they formerly criticized. They did not, however, abandon their new ideas about spirituality. In subsequent decades, they continued to use this term as it became a staple in the United States and beyond. At the turn of the millennium, the Gallup organization began to use the term in its polls where it asked Americans if they identify as spiritual or religious. These polls revealed that while a minority of the nation embraced this designation, the term was a part of American vernacular. As evidenced by more recent polls, it's a term that people increasingly embrace today.

Spirituality Reconsidered

That we live in a culture where the rhetoric of spirituality is common does not, however, mean the term is without its problems. One problem with the term is that "spirituality" is a catch-all term with a wide range of meanings and definitions. Some of these definitions overlap, but some are quite different. If they share anything, it's the underlying assumption that spirituality exists and is separate from religion. Beyond that, definitions of spirituality are quite diverse, and these various definitions fail to isolate spirituality as a distinct phenomenon.

Consider one study that sought to distinguish spirituality from religion. The researchers who organized this study and who wrote an academic paper describing their research assumed that spirituality exists and that it is separate from religion. Their research highlights many of the problems with the idea that spirituality is about spirituality. First, it follows a common pattern of using circular logic to define the term. To understand this criticism, consider that we use circular logic when we have limited information and we invoke that information to prove our point (while ignoring competing or contradictory information). For example, if I eat three tart apples, using circular logic, I can argue that all apples are tart. By this logic, I "know" that all apples are tart because my data set of three apples "proves" my point. The problem is that there are other apples that I'm ignoring. Apples can be sweet, they can be sour, or if they're rotting, they can taste metallic. In this example, my argument begins with the limited data set that I use to "prove" my point. People who invoke the rhetoric of spirituality often use circular logic, as evidenced by the aforementioned study that sought to distinguish spirituality from religion.

In their study, they asked their research subjects "to describe a situation in which you felt a strong connection with a higher power or a spiritual presence" (Miller et al. 2019, 2333). This instruction uses circular logic because it assumes its object of study (spiritual) to prove that it exists. They're basically asking people to describe spirituality by using the rhetoric of spirituality. A possible response to this instruction might be "I experienced spirituality when I encounter spirituality or spiritual presences." Another scholar similarly used circular logic when, after saying that it is difficult to define spirituality, he wrote that "spirituality comprises multiple dimensions that exist internally or become externally manifest through behaviours" (Lepherd 2014, 566). This scholar uses an intellectual sleight of hand to distract us from the fact that he simultaneously uses his object of study (spirituality) to reference it. As evidenced by these two examples, this is a common problem for people who discuss spirituality or who attempt to define it by referencing it. The fact that we can invent a term and describe some things using that term doesn't mean that the term we are using is legitimate.

These examples reveal another problem with the rhetoric of spirituality insofar as people who claim to be spiritual fail to identify with any precision how allegedly spiritual things are distinct from religion, culture, or other ideological systems. Consider the aforementioned study that sought to distinguish religion from spirituality. When they asked their research subjects to describe spiritual states, they said that "spiritual states are those that through a felt-sense connect you to something bigger than oneself, a oneness, or strong force which may be experienced as an energy, force, higher power, G-d, deity or transcendent figure or consciousness" (2333). The first problem with this definition of spiritual states is that it, too, uses circular logic. Additionally, one might simply reject this definition of a spiritual state (there are lots people out there who might say, "I wouldn't define it that way"), in which case the entire argument falls flat. If we accept, however, this definition of spiritual states, it encompasses a wide range of experiences. According to this definition, spirituality connects us to something "bigger than ourselves." But we, as humans, are always connected to things bigger than ourselves: families, schools, cities, nations, and so on. This idea of imagined connection to something bigger would apply to nationalism, to our fraternities or sororities, to the bond we feel with our families, to our connections with sports teams, to our connections with bands and musicians, or to any other imagined connections that most people are reluctant to classify as spiritual connections—if we applied it consistently, almost anything social would be "spiritual" on such a definition.

We can identify another potential problem with this definition of spiritual states because it concludes that spiritual states connect us to an "energy or force" that is bigger than oneself. By this definition, gravity induces a spiritual state. After all, it undoubtedly is bigger than me, I feel connected to gravity, and it has power over my life. No one, to our knowledge, has argued that gravity is spiritual, but definitions of spirituality and spiritual states that are so vague, if we apply them literally, would make gravity spiritual. Additionally, when swimming in the ocean, I would definitely feel connected to a large wave that pulls me underwater. By this definition of spiritual states, temporarily being held under water appears to be a spiritual state. Taking this train of thought to its logical conclusion, perhaps drowning is the ultimate spiritual experience?

An additional problem with this definition of spiritual states is that, if we accept this definition, it fails to distinguish how spirituality is different from religion. After all, a connection to "something bigger than oneself" sounds like the way people tend to describe religion. A connection with "an energy, force, higher power, G-d, deity or transcendent figure, or consciousness" similarly sounds like common descriptions of religion. To be clear, our argument is not that so-called spiritual states are actually religious states; rather, our argument is that there is nothing distinct about so-called spiritual states or spirituality that is not commonly associated with religion. If we are to distinguish them, we'll need a more precise definition, and those who claim to be spiritual but not religious rarely make the effort, or when they do, they create definitions that contradict each other's definitions.

Consider also that individual spirituality is often juxtaposed with organized religion or religious communities. By this logic, meditation or yoga is spiritual. There are two issues with this assumption. First, these practices (whether private or in a group) are also associated with many religions, particularly Asian religions, and second, meditation and yoga are often *performed in groups*, undermining the idea that spirituality is inherently private. Additionally, admiration for nature is often associated with spirituality, but admiration for nature is also associated with many religions. We can continue down the list of things people commonly associate with spirituality, but the larger point remains that there is nothing about so-called spirituality that isn't also commonly associated with religion. On what grounds are they different, other than the fact that those claiming to be spiritual are simultaneously asserting some sort of superiority?

Another criticism is that scholars have repeatedly demonstrated that what passes as spirituality is linked to capitalist consumption. "Spirituality" is a multi-billion-dollar industry. People who identify as SBNR routinely invest large amounts of money in their allegedly spiritual practices. Yoga mats, meditation cushions, alters, crystals, tarot cards, spiritual retreats, spiritual massages, beads, necklaces, and clothing are some of the more common expenses associated with spirituality and with spiritual disciplines or exercises. Generally speaking, when someone pursues what they call a spiritual path, they start spending money. In other words, most of us spend money every day on a host of goods and services. Labeling some of it as spirituality is the result of our attempt to justify some of it by invoking its sacredness.

To some extent, there's nothing obviously wrong with spending money on one's hobbies, other than that we're possibly being exploited when handing over large sums of cash for things we're infatuated with because they've been called "spiritual." However, arguably much of this consumption is colored by a subtle form of racism that scholars call "orientalism" or "orientalist stereotypes." The concept of orientalism was first explored by Edward Said in his book with the same name: *Orientalism*. There Said argued that European literature and history throughout the modern period was saturated with a systematic set of assumptions about fundamental differences between "the orient"—that is, "the East"—and "the occident"—that is, "the West." Those in Europe developed stereotypes about themselves by imagining themselves as superior to those in other parts of the world: "European identity [was] a superior one in comparison with all the non-European peoples and cultures" (Said 1978: 7). Orientalism assumed that the West was rational, dynamic and changing, and more civilized, while the East—especially Islam—was less rational and perhaps more mystical, stuck in the past, static, and unchanging, and lacked civilization. While Said's focus was on European Islamophobia, other scholars have looked at how in the nineteenth and twentieth centuries, stereotypes about "the orient" started to accumulate some positive associations, particularly when it came to Indian and Asian religious traditions. Hinduism and Buddhism, for instance, begin to be viewed as superior to Western religions in some senses. Western religions apparently emphasized rationality and objectively true doctrine, conformity to social rules, and external authority, while so-called Eastern religions emphasized mysticism and subjective experience, individualism rather than social conformity, and a focus on finding truth within rather than turning to external authorities outside oneself. While such arguably positive stereotypes might be less damaging than the negative, Islamophobic ones Said focused on, *they are still stereotypes.* As Richard King puts it in his book *Orientalism and Religion: Postcolonial Theory, India and 'The Mystic East,'* "there are in fact a number of heterogeneous facets to Indian religions and . . . not all of these are what we might call 'mystical'" (King 1999:4). If we let our assumptions about "Eastern" religions frame the way we perform our studies, we're liable to find what we want to find—and we'll miss all the evidence that, for instance, some Indian religious traditions might very well emphasize rationality, objectively true doctrine, conformity to social rules, and external authority.

The last criticism of spirituality we want to address is the fact that many forms of "spirituality" seem designed to encourage people to passively accept the status quo. Many—although clearly not all—books on "spirituality" encourage individuals to transform themselves above all else, rather than the social context in which they reside. If you are unhappy with your job, the solution is not to change your job or change the conditions under which you are working, but rather to *change yourself so that you experience the existing conditions in a positive rather than negative way.* As Craig Martin notes in *Capitalizing Religion: Ideology and the Opiate of the Bourgeoisie,* Lewis Richmond's book on Buddhism for the workplace argues that we should never get upset at any unfair treatment or injustice at work; those injustices are a good thing because they give us an opportunity to change ourselves so that we experience injustice as a good thing rather than a bad thing (see Martin 2014: 127–34). Spirituality guru Karen Berg argues that any suffering we experience is always our own fault; she explicitly claims that if a woman's husband is cheating on her, it is always *her fault*—such a woman must spiritually change herself rather than expect her philandering husband to change his behavior (see Martin 2014: 145–50). In Eckhart Tolle's bestselling book on spirituality, *The Power of Now*, he explicitly claims that we always cause our own suffering and that if a woman's husband is physically abusive, it is her fault and she must change herself rather than expect him to change. He even goes so far as to say that we cause our own physical illnesses. Because we are the cause of our own suffering, we must always change ourselves instead of the world (see Martin 2014: 150–5). Jeremy Carrette and Richard King, in *Selling Spirituality: The Silent Takeover of Religion*, demonstrate that many books on spirituality teach a form of individualism according to which any problem "is always your problem, deal with yourself, not with society" (Carrette and King 2005: 107). This is a "'feel good' spirituality for the urban and the affluent and. . . has nothing to say to the poor and the marginalized society, other than offering a regime of compliance" (107). For these forms of spirituality, the only thing we need to do for those people in Detroit whose water is polluted with lead is to tell them to change themselves, or to tell those women who are victims of sexual assault to change their outlook on life, or to tell those people who are disadvantaged by racism to learn to love the people who oppress them.

In summary, some of the technical problems with the concept of spirituality include circular definitions, or the fact that definitions are so vague that, strictly speaking, "spirituality" overlaps with those things people would like to distinguish it from, like "organized religion." However, beyond the technical problems we have arguably social problems: some forms of spirituality seem designed to line the pockets of those who sell "spiritual" goods like crystals, yoga mats, and candles with Chinese letters scrawled on them; some forms of spirituality are tinged with deeply problematic stereotypes about people from India and Asia; and some forms of spirituality teach people to accept the status quo and see any form of suffering as an opportunity to change oneself, rather than the causes in the world that might contribute to that suffering in the first place.

Conclusion

Undergraduates (and Americans more broadly) grow up in a nation and a culture where the rhetoric of spirituality is ubiquitous. We see it on social media, we read about it, we hear it, and we purchase products related to our own alleged spirituality and spiritual journeys. In this essay, however, we have argued that "spirituality" is arguably about other things: claiming a sense of superiority, reproducing stereotypes about so-called Asian religions, capitalist consumption, or teaching people to accept the status quo. As should be clear, we are not necessarily criticizing so-called spirituality and spiritual exercises;

rather, we're highlighting how the rhetoric of spirituality is problematic insofar as it claims to be distinct from religion and other aspects of culture, yet it lacks a stable definition, so-called spiritual "things" are virtually indistinguishable from religion and culture, and it appears to have unexplored associations. From this perspective, spirituality is not about spirituality; rather, like all language, it is embedded in larger political and cultural currents that people use to advance their various (and often competing) agendas.

5

"Eastern Religions Are More Spiritual than Western Religions"

Ting Guo

This chapter reflects on the cliché that considers Eastern religions as more spiritual than Western ones. I first use the example of Buddhism as a religion that has long been appropriated and used to depict Asia as the exotic other in the cultural imagination of the West, with an apparent appreciation of the religion's peacefulness in contrast with Western military aggression, capitalism, or political corruption. In today's context, Buddhism and other Asian religions are further considered as the paradigmatic ideology of late capitalism while perpetuating the depiction of Asians as the cultural and religious other in the postsecular West. Such representation of Eastern religions leaves Asia out of modernity, ignores the complex modernizing process in Asia, and reinforces a binary framework of religion as either strictly Eastern or Western. Using the framework of diffused and engaged religion—the way in which religious institutions, theologies, and rituals are intimately merged with sociopolitical life—I demonstrate how religions are an integral part of Asian modernity, social movements, and official politics. I further demonstrate the global dimension of "Asian religions" and how some "Western" religions are Eastern religions too. Quite often, these religions could be more productively studied in terms of the *connections* across spatial and temporal contexts, as people share a vast repertoire of ideas and practices around the world. In this way, we can study Asian religions while avoiding the essentializations of them from both state reinventions and orientalist imaginations.

The Cliché: Orientalist Representations
of Asian Religions in the West[1]

First, Buddhism has long been used to depict Asia as the exotic and yet utopian other in the cultural imagination of the West. This is what Edward Said defines as "orientalism": that in addition to being the colonies, the Orient also constitutes the "deepest and most recurring images of the other" for the West and justifies its dominating restructuring and authority over the Orient (Said 2014). For instance, early Buddhist films in the United States, such as D. H. Griffith's *Broken Blossoms* (also known as *The Yellow Man and the Girl*; 1919) and Frank Capra's *Lost Horizon* (1937), set out a framework that sees Buddhism as "a marker of otherness" and "inassimilable difference" Suh 2015, 29). *Broken Blossoms* tells the story of an idealistic Chinese man who wanted to share Buddhist teachings with Westerners, ended up in disillusion because of the violence in Western society that he encountered, and took his own life in front of a makeshift Buddhist shrine. *Lost Horizon* is based on the novel by the English writer James Hilton and foregrounds Shangri-La, a fictional utopia near Himalaya as the symbol of faraway dreamlands in Western imaginations; Shangri-La serves as the context for his adventure fantasy of Western diplomats encountering indigenous political upheavals. The actual location and histories of this distant land were intentionally left out to show an out-of-context ideal to steer the audience's imagination.

Asian religions in Western representations also depict some kind of spiritual wisdom or enlightenment that are alternatives to Christianity or Western ideologies, often in an ahistorical manner, that is, without historical context or understanding of its changing dynamics or even nature. For instance, *Lost Horizon* created the utopian land Shangri-La and reinforced a cultural trend of imagining Tibet, Himalaya, India and other Asian places as spiritual places frozen in an ideal time that are longed for but unattainable, regardless of the modern sociopolitical transformations of those societies and the changing manifestations of religions in those places. Decades later, Marvel Comics created characters such as the Ancient One and Black Priests to represent similar magical powers or ancient Eastern wisdom.

Moreover, both *Broken Blossoms* and *Lost Horizon* were also notorious for their paradoxical portrayal of Asians as the "yellow peril," despite representing Eastern religions as distinctively peaceful to contrast Western military aggression or political corruption (for systematic accounts of the "yellow peril," see Frayling 2014; Keevak 2011; and Huang 2010). In this way, the representation of Buddhism in early Western films was a double-edged sword that acknowledged as well as racialized and exoticized Eastern religions. According to this racializing and exoticizing logic, Eastern religions have to be embodied in an Asian body in order to manifest its difference as the cultural other. However, in reality, such racialization of Asian religions persists and is often carried out by whitewashing, that is, casting white actors and actresses to play Asian characters. With whitewashing, white culture continues to dominate cultural landscapes and overrides the voices of both Asians from Asia and ethnic minorities within Western societies. The Caucasian American actor Richard Barthelmess portrayed the Chinese man in *Broken Blossoms*, Anglo-Saxon actors played the Asian characters in *Lost Horizon*, and generations of white actors from Harry Agar Lyons, Christopher Lee, to Nicolas Cage portrayed the notorious Fu Manchu, a mysterious Asian supervillain created by the English writer Sax Rohmer. Even in recent cinema, the British actress Tilda Swinton played the role of the Ancient One in the Marvel film *Doctor Strange*. Notably, the cover of Sax Rohmer's first novel of Fu Manchu used lotus flower, beads, Asian deities, robe, incense, and other objects and styles commonly associated with Eastern religions to depict a mysterious Orient in a highly racialized manner. The representation of Eastern religions in Western literary and popular culture has both contributed to and reinforced racism and the tradition of whitewashing, reducing them to a stereotype and erasing more dynamic Asian characters from both cultural representation and social imaginations.

In today's social media age, the consumption of Eastern religions from home deco to yoga studios, from Instagram videos to celebrity gurus, has further produced a cliché of Asian religions as the spiritual alternative to Western capitalism, but only to be consumed.[2] Famous brands such as Lululemon are known for capitalizing on yogic practice with a consumerist model of discipline and self-care, which some have called "spiritual capitalism" (no author 2014). Lululemon's website even specifically introduces "yoga" as a kind of ancient wisdom from the Sanskrit root for the spirit and physical body and that "Yoga has evolved over thousands of years to embrace a wide range of styles and disciplines and it's a popular activity for athletes, children, and seniors. . . Yoga energizes our bodies and calms our minds" (no author 2022). As scholars have argued, Lululemon branding consistently refers to vague, homogenizing, and orientalist concepts of Eastern spiritualities that instrumentalize yogic practices, while reinforcing Western ideologies of health along with personal, bodily, and market performance (see Lavrence and Lozanski 2014; Bird 2014; Jain 2020; Arjana 2020; Putcha 2020 among many others). In academia, too, scholars often refer to Eastern religions as the ideological other to Western capitalism or teach Eastern religions in an "essentialized and distorted" form that emphasizes nonviolence (Owen 2011, 263). In Slovenian philosopher Slovaj Žižek's words, Buddhism is "establishing itself as the hegemonic ideology of global capitalism" (Žižek 2006, 252) as part of the "strange exchange" (Žižek 2001) between East and the West, as Buddhism and other Asian religions have effectively become the new ideology for global capitalism and threaten the legacy of Judeo-Christianity in the postsecular West. Žižek recognizes the ways in which Western Buddhism is reduced to a kind of pop culture phenomenon that preaches "inner distance and indifference" toward market competition, while at the same time being arguably the most efficient way for us fully to participate in capitalist dynamics while maintaining the appearance of mental sanity—in short, the paradigmatic ideology of late capitalism (Žižek 2003, 26). Philosopher Eske Møllgaard vividly illustrates Žižek's argument in a parody, that Western Buddhism is the lifestyle best suited to our age of global capitalism, the age where hedonism and asceticism are combined: "We indulge in a double-mocha-latte, but it has to be decaf" (Møllgaard 2008, 169).

How Does This Cliché Happen?

The cliché that Eastern religions are more spiritual is certainly a result of orientalism, but it is also co-constituted by both Western and Asian intellectual and political elites who are in a more powerful position to produce cultural imaginaries and define modernity. Moreover, this cliché also stems from the changing perception of "spirituality" as something different from institutional Christianity in contemporary Christian-secular West.

At the root of this cliché, Eastern religions are viewed as more spiritual because Asian religions are imagined out of context, without any regard to how Asia actually evolved and changed throughout history, especially in the modern era and with respect to transnational immigration. Such ahistorical imagination leaves Asia out of modernity and stuck in the past and ignores the very real and very complex modernizing process in Asia. Accordingly, Asian people are also imagined as exotic and unmodern when Asia is depicted as remote and ahistorical, as we have seen from the examples above about how Hollywood represents Asia as an exotic utopia and Asians as racialized others.

In *Orientalism and Religion: Postcolonial Theory, India, and "The Mystic East,"* Richard King traces such orientalism to the European Enlightenment, when the notion of "the Mystic East" became a prevalent theme within Western understandings of places such as India, while the West established a system of scientific knowledge for modern thought (King 1999). The Enlightenment, a philosophical and social revolution, became the foundation and authority for not only the West but other parts of the world as well. In this way, the cliché that Eastern religions are more spiritual also implies the idea that Eastern religions and Asia in general being irrelevant, less advanced, less modern, or less scientific.

This cliché is often used by *both* Western and Asian elites. In *The Religious Question of Modern China*, David Palmer and Vincent Goosaert point out that when China was in an "ideological crisis" at the turn of the century, destroying religion of imperial China and inventing a new place for religion in the nation-state were important modernizing projects (Palmer and Goosaert 2004, 43, 54). In the name of modernization, Chinese religions began to be defined as "superstitious" as intellectuals imported notions of "religion" and "secular" from the Christian-secular model, with an entire rejection of China's traditional religious heritage, most notably during the New Culture movement in the 1910s and 1920s (2004, 54, 68). Since the founding of the People's Republic of China (PRC) in 1949, another secularizing movement further crushed the religious ecology in China, namely the Cultural Revolution (1966–7), when religious activities and cultural traditions including Confucianism were suppressed and temples, halls, and churches destroyed (Kao 2009, 171–88).[3] Historian Lian Xi also reveals that missionaries in the nineteenth and early twentieth century found science plus Christianity to be a useful formula to recruit followers. They toured China with modern technologies to prove the West's superiority to Chinese intellectuals (Lian 2013, 70–87). In doing so, they deemed China as more backward not only scientifically but also religiously, as Chinese religions were considered not enlightened by modernity. For those missionaries/scientists, Christianity was the only savior for China as a nation, as it represented modernity and democracy, while Chinese religions were merely superstitious without a powerful system (2013: 82). Similarly, Florence C. Hsia in *Sojourners in a Strange Land: Jesuits and Their Scientific Missions in Late Imperial China* shows how missionaries capitalized on Chinese intellectual elites' curiosity of Western technology and began to argue how such modern progress was an integral part of Christianity in the West (Hsia 2009). As a result, a binary framework differentiated an advanced, Christian Modernity in the West from a spiritual but traditional, backward East.

The presumed superiority of Christianity and the Christian-secular model remains with us in the postsecular age, as the model of Western secularism is considered a "globally shared form" of modern liberal national-political structuration (Mahmood 2015, 2). Writing on Islam in postcolonial Egypt, scholars such as Saba Mahmood and Lila Abu-Lughod have observed the impact of secularism as a Western ideology on both the global perception of religions and the religious dynamics in the non-Western world (Mahmood 2016 and Abu-Lughod 2013). Quite often the religious manifestations and dynamics of non-Western societies are seen as the result of incomplete secularization—as if they are behind on progress—even though, as Mahmood notes, modern secular governance itself can intensify as well as transform interfaith inequalities and is therefore itself arguably "backward" in some ways (Mahmood 2015, 2). In other words, the cliché that Eastern religions are more spiritual also implies a prejudice that the East is insufficiently secularized, hence less liberal and less modern.

This cliché is also a result of the changing understanding of what counts as "spiritual" in Western world. Since the New Age movement, which arguably emerged in the 1960s' counterculture era (see Faber 1996 and Heelas 1996), the term "spirituality" has often been celebrated as a differentiation and a moving-away from institutional religion, that is, usually Christianity, toward what are considered to be "alternative" beliefs and practices within the supposedly secular landscape in the West. If we look closer, however, the elements attributed to the formation of the rise of spirituality are contradictory. Some of the major components of the "new spiritualities" are ironically part of existing non-Christian religious and cultural traditions. Elements and aspects of, for example, Buddhism, Hinduism, Islam, and Daoism are commonly embraced, though their key beliefs and ideas have been rearranged to different degrees. In response, scholars such as Colin Campbell have problematized the New Age adoption of non-Western traditional religious elements. In his "A New Age Theodicy for a New Age," Campbell takes the example of *samsara* and *karma*, terms that are, historically, connected to the claim that life is suffering and escape from this world is the ultimate goal of life; Campbell notes that "what has been a profoundly pessimistic view of the human condition in India has been twisted into an upbeat optimism—from reincarnation as a terrible fate, to reincarnation as an endless enjoyment of self-enchanting possibilities" (Campbell 2001, 193). What Campbell points out is only one example of Western appropriation and (mis)interpretation of concepts from other cultural and religious traditions and how these misinterpretations are uncritically regrouped into New Age thought. In other words, in borrowing from various religious traditions within the construct of the "new spirituality," it contradicts its own claim of "traditional religions" "giving way to holistic spirituality" (Heelas and Woodhead 2005, 2). These non-Western religious traditions are considered as either more "subjective" or more spiritual, because their subjective and spiritual elements could be freely drawn on without institutional baggage, because they are considered foreign.

Stereotyping is often mutual, of course. For instance, King points out that orientalist essentialism has resulted in stereotypes about the West as well as the East (King 1999, 3). However, Eastern stereotypes do not have the power to reinforce Eastern dominance over Western nations. Behind the West's spiritual imaginations of Eastern religions, lies the issue of modernization hierarchy where the complexity of modernity in the non-Western world gets neglected.

"Asian Religions" as Diffused and Engaged World Religions

How do we change this cliché about Asian religions?

1. Diffused and engaged religion

The first couple of notions to consider is the ideas of "diffused" and "engaged" religion. These two notions will help us understand how the spiritual and the secular are not separated, which further helps illuminate the modern transformations of Asian societies and Asian religions.

In studying the religious role in Chinese societies, sociologist C. K. Yang famously proposed the notion of diffused religion in response to the question, "Is there religion in China?," to which he answered that various Chinese religions are diffused in practice insofar as their institutions are less distinct or not separate from each other; therefore, it might be difficult to distinguish one from another.[4] For instance, rituals conducted at home often mix different religions, including folk religions, Buddhism, and Daoism, while people who conduct these rituals may deny being religious when asked (see Chau 2005). At the same time, their religious functions are performed through and by sociopolitical institutions such as the kinship system, the imperial state, and communal rituals (Yang 1961, 304); therefore, it might be difficult to tell where Chinese religions are on the surface as Chinese religions do not look the same way as Christianity in historical Europe.

This notion of diffused religion is related to the notion of "engaged" religion, which refers to and demonstrates how religion in Asia, in particular those considered "peaceful," related to a way of life without contexts, are actively involved in political and social changes. I borrow this notion from "Engaged Buddhism," which emerged in twentieth-century Asia in response to liberation movements. Largely a decentralized movement throughout different times and places, this term was coined during the Vietnam War by the Vietnamese monk Thich Nhat Hanh, who cofounded the School of Youth for Social Service in order to train young Buddhists to serve the needs of the Vietnamese people, particularly in the countryside (King 2009, 4). Engaged Buddhism became "a vehicle capable of giving voice to the people's political aspirations and bringing down national governments" (2009, 1). In part, this development was a response to the charge that Buddhism has been too passive and aloof. In East Asia, scholars have also shown how Tzu Chi, a Buddhist organization led by nuns, has been leading modern feminist, anticolonial, and environmental movements (see Huang 2009; Yao 2012; Lee and Han 2015; Lee and Han 2016; and Lee and Han 2021).

I use these notions to show how religions in Asia have been modernized, as well as to describe the interdynamics between religion and sociopolitical changes in modern Asia, including the way in which Asian religions manifest in and are essentialized by state apparatuses as well as their active participation in modernization processes and social movements. For instance, the current PRC regime has been appropriating Confucianism in authoritarian governance, state policies, patriotic education, popular culture, and foreign strategies. State propaganda has repeatedly emphasized filial piety and other Confucian traditions as being essential to the maintenance of social stability. Such reinvention of Confucianism marks a return to a more conservative and traditional heteronormative society in which obedience is valued as a social and political morality, while authoritarian power is reconfigured as political leaders appear as firm but benevolent parents, while dissidents are cast as children requiring discipline (see Guo 2021). In reality, however, Confucianism is historically an evolving, dynamic system that absorbed various schools, including Legalism, a school that emphasized state control, while retaining the outward appearance of a Confucian framework. Confucianism is also appropriated to create a sense of identity and cultural superiority of the majority Han ethnicity. The Han, the ethnicity behind what is commonly known as "the Chinese," are recognized by the PRC as the national majority and the core of China's multiethnic nation, represented or embodied by Confucianism, which became formalized as a state ideology during the Han dynasty (202 BCE–220 CE). In reality, "Chinese" is not a race or ethnicity and what is known as China today has not always been ruled by the Han. However, over the centuries, Confucian culture and institutions persisted, often through Sinicization, meaning "integration" or assimilation of different races and ethnicities into Han Chinese Confucianism (see Schluessel 2020). Today, Confucianism is blended into official ideology as the core of national identity and is used to differ from "foreign" traditions such as liberalism as well as legitimizing patriarchal authoritarianism (Bell 2014, 33). In this way, the reinvention of Confucianism hypocrizes the state's heavy-handed control of the people, especially ethnic minorities, women, activists, and other marginalized groups.

Diffused and engaged religion also manifest in social movements. In 2019, diffused elements of Daoism, Buddhism, and folk religions were prominent in support of the Anti-Extradition Law Amendment Bill (anti-ELAB), prohibiting Hong Kong government from extraditing dissidents to Mainland China who took over the sovereignty of Hong Kong since 1997 (see Chow 1995). The presence of these groups included a makeshift shrine outside a central shopping mall, where a young protestor died the night before a scheduled march. Over two million people offered flowers, candles, incense, and snacks to the "shrine," all elements commonly seen at ancestral memorials, Buddhist and Daoist temples, and funerals. *Namo Amitābha* 南無阿彌陀佛,

a well-known Han Chinese Buddhist chant, also played in the background. Wong Tai Sin 黃大仙, a local deity and famous tourist attraction, also became a famous figure for protest art against the police's use of teargas, symbolizing a celebration of Hong Kong's own guardian and divine protection. Religion also underpinned the earlier Occupy Central with Love and Peace movement in 2014, as pastors led prayers in more privileged Central and Admiralty districts and shrines for folk religion's god of war and justice, Guan Gong, 關公, were set up in Mongkok, traditionally dwelled by refugees and working-class Chinese. These are all examples of how religions in Hong Kong have diffused into secular institutions and engaged with sociopolitical movements, manifesting the pursuit of democracy, justice, and freedom today on the grassroots, noninstitutional level and contrasting the out-of-context "spiritual" stereotype of Eastern religions.[5]

2. So-called "Western" religions are "Asian religions" too and many "Asian religions" are global religions.

My second observation is that so-called "Western" religions are Asian religions too and many "Asian religions" are global religions as they emigrate with communities and develop transnationally. Quite often, these religions could be more productively studied in terms of the connections across spatial and temporal contexts. In order to better illustrate this point, I find Henrietta Harrison's *The Missionary's Curse and Other Tales from a Chinese Catholic Village* (2013) an excellent reference. Harrison begins her inquiry from the perennial debate over whether Christianity and "Chinese culture" are compatible or whether Christianity could be considered a Chinese religion. It has been widely noted that Christianity in China—particularly rural China—has been highly localized in terms of church architecture, the liturgy, and many other aspects of worship and religious practice. At the same time, many nonlocal forces are at work, connecting Chinese Christianity to the wider Christian world. Both Chinese culture and global Christianity are diverse and constantly changing. Simultaneously, many aspects of global Christianity have changed: Catholics in Europe today take part in a very different set of practices and rituals than they did in the nineteenth century. Being part of a world religion inherently involves a desire to share the ideas and practices of people elsewhere in the world (Harrison 2013). This demonstrates how people share a "vast and intensely debated repertoire of ideas and practices" around the world (2013, 207). In 2019 Hong Kong, the involvement of Christianity also caught the attention of major local and international media and Christian hymn-themed "Sing Hallelujah to the Lord" and "Glory to Hong Kong" were deemed as the unofficial anthems of the movement. Regarding the transnational aspect of Chinese religions, Richard Madsen and Elijah Siegler point out how Chinese religions go through constant changes with migrants and diasporas, and Chinese religious terms such as *fengshui, yin yang*, and Tao/*dao* have become common lexicons around the world beyond the boundaries of Chinese communities (Madsen and Siegler 2011, 227). In "The Religious Composition of the Chinese Diaspora, Focusing on Canada," Skirbekk et al. have also pointed out the diversity of Eastern religions practiced by diasporas (Skirbekk et al. 2012).

Conclusion

Writing on the representation of Islam in the West, anthropologist Lila Abu-Lughod remarks:

> If we were to listen and look, we might be forced to take account of contexts that are not as disconnected from our worlds and our own lives as we think. These contexts are shaped by global politics, international capital, and modern state institutions. (Abu-Lughod, 2013, 6)

Such is an important voice in recognizing the nuances beyond East versus West binaries. The same principle should be applied to the study on other "Eastern religions," too; that is, we do not refer to them as "more spiritual" or other essentialized forms, but, rather, study how religions are developed within, across, and beyond geopolitical boundaries, how powers appropriate religion, and how traditions came to be embedded and developed at different historical moments over time. In other words, we need to caution against two forms of essentializations: the states' reinvention of religious traditions and the orientalist imagination of religion in Asia. Asian religions evolve like any other cultural traditions; we shouldn't essentialize them as unchanging. Rather than seeking some essentialized spiritual "authenticity," we should always look for the historical and sociopolitical factors that shape many aspects of religious manifestations.

6

"Each Religion Has an Authentic, Unchanging Core"

David G. Robertson

In June 2018, the Supreme Court of the United States ruled in favor of Jack Phillips, a Colorado baker who refused to bake a cake for a same-sex wedding. The ruling commented that the First Amendment "guarantee[s] that our laws be applied in a manner that is neutral toward religion." For many scholars with an interest in how religion is dealt with in legal contexts—and perhaps even constructed by legislation as Tisa Wenger argues (2009)—this was a key debate, putting gay rights head-to-head against religious liberty. Phillips commented that "I didn't want to use my artistic talents to create something that went against my Christian faith. . . . The Bible says, 'In the beginning there was male and female'" (de Vogue 2018). Both these arguments present the issue as core to Christianity, and indeed, for Phillips, the two positions seem utterly entwined and nonnegotiable.

When in July 2021, the same Supreme Court rejected a similar case brought by Barronelle Stutzman, a Washington state florist who refused to provide flowers for a same-sex wedding (Swoyer 2021), the debate on how Christians should regard homosexuality immediately reopened. The National Catholic Reporter argued that God is concerned with how we treat the poor and vulnerable, and so an "authentic" Christian would not have refused to sell the cake to the couple (Perriello 2017). For Michael Coren, writing in the *Globe and Mail*, authentic Christianity is "the opposite of 'virtue signaling,'" but instead living with compassion for your neighbor and yourself (Coren 2021). But for Marc Greenwood, in a letter published in the Sun Journal, "Authentic Christianity requires courage"—the courage to break laws which prevent one from discriminating against homosexuals, apparently, citing Martin Luther King to support this position (Greenwood 2021).

In all these comments, the appeal to "authentic" Christianity positions the writer as representing (or at least, defending) the true core of the religion. That core is taken as something which remains, and has always remained, constant, even in changing times and different contexts (as shown by Phillips' citing of a 5000-year-old Jewish text). No one seems to question at any point either that there *is* in fact a single Christianity that has a clear set of things one *must* believe or that Phillips had any choice in whether to act. And these assumptions go hand in hand—if there are no essential, core Christian beliefs, then Phillips' identification as a Christian is not contingent on whatever he decides to do.

In fact, this conception of religions as having an unchanging, authentic core is a key claim in how they are understood in popular culture, political discourse, interfaith dialogue, and even academic work, especially through the tendency to classify religions according to such essential differences, often referred to as the World Religions Paradigm. Unpacking the claim reveals that it is actually more complex than it might at first seem. From a critical perspective, claims about what constitutes the core of a religion—the "sine qua non," the "that without which" one cannot claim it to be a member—is a matter for insiders, rather than scholars. But demonstrating that insider claims or definitions about this have changed over time, on the other hand, is a task for the scholar, requiring care to ensure that one is not interpreting earlier material through the lens of contemporary understanding.

But it's even more complicated than this. There is widespread disagreement even today as to what this unchanging core actually is, especially among the members, as the anecdote I began with shows. And this disagreement is not a modern phenomenon either, some new breakdown of the true faith in the face of secularism, or an attack on "traditional values," as Greenwood's letter suggested (2021). In fact, historically speaking, the idea of a core of teaching or practices or even experiences that can be regarded as uniquely and consistently belonging to each single religion, person to person, unchangingly throughout history and across the globe is demonstrably false. This is not just me, a critical scholar, saying that; even the Church of England Bishop and theologian S. W. Sykes writes that such claims amount to little more than "rhetorical devices to commend the depth or fundamental character of a specific investigation" (1971, 291). That is to say, their purpose is to lend the speaker authority, by implying their special access to the *true core* of the tradition.

Ultimately, the question of authenticity is not a disinterested evaluation, but a normative one, which must refer to some-or-other idea of what that religion *should* be. An authentic Christian is a *real* Christian (or Buddhist, or

Muslim, or etc.). But no one ever thinks *their* denomination is inauthentic. Yet by appealing to our idea of what the religion should be as though it were *the* "authentic, unchanging core," we legitimize it, as well as gaining social capital for ourselves as a representative of this essence, and the metaphysical power or divine order it represents.

As such, insider claim about this "authentic unchanging core" leads us into *essentialism*, and the claim that there is some irreducible essence to each religion. While this idea was central to the academic study of religion for a long time (which we will examine in more detail later), scholars approaching religion from a critical perspective consider this claim problematic. In some disciplines, reference to essences is a straightforward matter, such as in chemistry, where carbon or gold has specific and testable atomic structures, or in mathematics where each number has a specific and constant value. Categories based on such quantifiable qualities are sometimes called "natural kinds," whereas categories like religion are "social kinds"; that is, they are not categorized according to properties which exist independently of human beings and their language systems (Josephson-Storm 2021, 91–7). Indeed, in a social scientific context, such claims about the essence of religion(s) often slide into metaphysical speculation.

Religious Essence in Popular Manifestation

The idea that religions have distinct and unchanging essences is a fundamental aspect of how the general public think about religion in the twenty-first century. We typically grow up thinking about a more-or-less discrete group of "World Religions" (usually Christianity, Islam, Judaism, Hinduism, and Buddhism, although Sikhism, Jainism, Daoism, and Baha'i often make an appearance), each of which is presented as having a symbol, a founder, a sacred book, and a distinct set of core beliefs. This is the so-called "World Religions Paradigm," the standard model for organizing and categorizing religions, which remains ubiquitous in politics, popular culture, and interfaith discourse, even as it has come under sustained and rigorous critique in scholarship (more on that soon). Anything falling outside of this model is either "indigenous" (and, by implication and genealogy, primitive) or a "cult" (and by implication, deviant, and dangerous).

Because the idea of World Religions—and indeed the concept of religion itself—developed in a predominantly Protestant context, we have tended to focus on beliefs as being the essence of each of these World Religions. "Buddhists," I have been told on a number of occasions (by non-Buddhists, of course), "are pacifists, and they believe in reincarnation." This is often qualified with a comment about how they don't believe in a God, at least not in the way that "we" do. The idea that Buddhists have ever been completely pacifist is a historical fantasy (see Jerryson and Juergensmeyer 2010 for examples). The Buddha's teachings, especially the Three Jewels and the Eightfold Path, are often presented as the core of Buddhism, especially in the West, where Buddhism has historically tended to be portrayed as a predominantly philosophical system. But studies of people across the world have shown that these doctrines are not of central importance to the majority who self-identify as Buddhists. The idea that the core of Buddhism is the aim of achieving Buddhahood only became a central concern for the majority of Buddhists after Mahayana Buddhism had been adopted in China. Ironically, we see that disagreement over what the (unchanging, eternal) core of the religion is lies at the root of the schism between Theravada and Mahayana—just as it was with the split in Christianity between Catholicism and Protestantism. Even then, there are still millions of Buddhists for whom this is not the central concern, even if in the West we tend to focus on the later developments, presenting Theravada Buddhism as an earlier—and by implication, more primitive—form. Even in China and Japan, however, Pure Land Buddhism, which revolves instead around devotion to different Buddhas and bodhisattvas, remains among the most popular forms. As with Hinduism, the philosophy of an elite was taken as the doctrine of the whole, and the religious lives of millions were ignored.

Nor is this an issue that is unique to Buddhism. In Christianity, Saint Paul clashed with Saint James over whether Christians could eat "idol meat" and whether they needed to be circumcised. In the fourth century, the Roman Emperor Constantine organized the Council of Nicaea in part because the church couldn't agree on a whole host of theological questions, including some that are often regarded as fundamental today, such as the nature of the Trinity and the divinity of Jesus. So even an apparently commonsense statement like "faith in Jesus" doesn't hold true at all times. "Faith in Jesus *as a God*" ("carmen Christo quasi deo di") was not universal in early Christianity, nor is it today. And it was only with the split between the Protestant churches and the Catholic Church, which followed Martin Luther's protestations, that faith came to be regarded as the core of authentic Christianity, rather than fealty to the church. Indeed, this was when the expression "the essence of Christianity" first appeared (Sykes 1971). Even so, we could say that establishing the core of Christianity has been a primary task of theology since its beginning.

Finding a core, essential belief to Judaism or Hinduism is even harder. But what we find in all these cases is the presentation by an elite group *as if* it were the core set of beliefs. In the case of Hinduism, this was the doctrines of the Brahmins, who were able to fit their ideas into the Christian mold—the

Vedas as their Bible; the Brahmins as Priests; Brahma, Siva, and Vishnu as their Trinity; and so on—at the expense of the vast majority of Hindus, whose ideas and practices had little if anything to do with this model and who in many cases did not even realize that they were Hindus until they were informed of this by the state.

The Politics of Essence/The Essence of Politics

This brings me neatly to the next point: the idea that religions have an essential core is an important part of political rhetoric. Perhaps the most obvious example of this was the discourse of authentic Islam, which emerged in Europe and North America in the early twenty-first century, in the wake of 9/11 and the resulting "War on Terror." In a political sense, the most obvious expressions of the War on Terror were the series of land invasions, missile strikes, and drone campaigns launched by the United States and its allies on supposedly "extremist" Islamic groups in Afghanistan, Iraq, Yemen, Syria, and other states. As I write this, the United States is in the process of a messy withdrawal from Afghanistan, but campaigns continue elsewhere, now twenty years after 9/11. There were social consequences, too, with Muslims coming under attack through legislation in different countries, including the infamous "no-fly list" in the United States, focusing almost exclusively on Middle Eastern Muslim-majority states, and France banning the wearing of full-face veils in April 2011. Media campaigns in the UK centered on the idea that Muslim groups were attempting to infiltrate schools (the "Trojan Horse" affair) and that organized gangs of Muslim men were abducting white girls, frequently presented their Islamic identity as a driver of "anti-Western" behaviors. These narratives—along with more conspiratorial versions like the so-called "Great Replacement" of European white Christians by Muslim immigrants—contributed in no small way to the rise of a new populist right-wing politics, culminating in the election of Donald Trump and the "Brexit" referendum in the UK in 2016. They also reinforced a perception of Islam as a monolithic, totalizing tradition, which was essentially violent and repressive and which demanded absolute fealty from its adherents.

On September 10, 2014, President Obama gave a major speech addressing the US's foreign policy in regard to terrorism. In it, he stated:

At this moment, the greatest threats come from the Middle East and North Africa, where radical groups exploit grievances for their own gain. And one of those groups is ISIL—which calls itself the "Islamic State." Now let's make two things clear: ISIL is not "Islamic." No religion condones the killing of innocents, and the vast majority of ISIL's victims have been Muslim. And ISIL is certainly not a state. (Obama 2014)

Following this, many politicians and broadcasters began referring to Daesh rather than ISIS (or ISIL) to avoid describing them as Islamic. Many Islamic groups also sought to distance themselves from ISIS, and so Islam from terrorism, in both the United States and the United Kingdom (see Karepetyan 2017; Townsend and McVeigh 2014; and Awad 2014). Scholars, too, sought to challenge prejudices and to correct the perception of Islam as incompatible with European and American liberalism (Hughes 2015, 1–4).

On the one hand, this move had the positive outcome that their Muslimness was no longer literally the first word of the acronym used to identify them, so it avoids reifying further the assumption that Islam is the primary cause of their violence. But it is problematic nonetheless to therefore say that it is not real religion, or real Islam, because it is violent, as though real religion is something that is fundamentally peaceful. This is another legacy of the colonial imposition of a normative Christian category, "religion." I say normative, because the idea of Christian societies as any more peaceful than any other is nonsense. The same goes for Islam or Buddhism, for that matter. In denying those Muslims who do not fit this "progressive," "multicultural" template, we actually do exactly what we are seeking to correct—erase all inner diversity to construct a one-sided, idealized version for political reasons (Hughes 2015, 3).

Furthermore, we can see that the "real" Islam in these cases is one that fits certain aspects of the model of religion that suits Western states—which is to say, a Christian, mostly Protestant, model in which notions of charity, peace, etc. are emphasized. Funnily enough, these particular values are probably more in common with Islamic and Christian moral teachings than some other traditions, though in this case, these differences are amplified and turned into the flash points. As important, however, is the post-Enlightenment and postcolonial worldview in which a particular form of secularism is encouraged, including free-market economies and private property. It may well be that the "real" Islam that Obama welcomes has a good deal to do with upholding these values as any theological differences.

"An Explosion of Data": Essences and Colonialism

By the seventeenth century, two factors were driving the emergence of the category "religion" as we understand it today, which is to say, as something plural (as in, different "religions") and a matter of personal identity. The first was the development of Protestantism, which was basically a theological movement that presented the essence of Christianity as faith, rather than the Church and its rituals, which was regarded as being the Catholic position. As such, it opened up new critiques of the Bible itself as text, and the Catholic interpretation thereof, and it is probably not overstating things to suggest that biblical studies as we know it today would not exist if not for these early Protestant theologians. This process of "intellectualization" encouraged the idea that a religion is a "system of beliefs," that is, as something predominantly taking place within the mind of the individual, rather than something more to do with community and collective practices—to whit, Catholicism. This in turn facilitated the move for religion to be understood as existing in the "private" sphere, rather than the public sphere—a tenet that was essential to the secularisms which emerged in France and the United States during the eighteenth century. We still see the ramifications of this playing out to this day in cases such as those of Jack Phillips and Barronelle Stutzman.

The second factor driving the modern, essentialized idea of religion was the colonial project. The concept of religions plural, and indeed, "world religions," was necessary "in response to an explosion of data" that was produced during the subjugation of ever more land by a few European powers during the eighteenth and nineteenth centuries. The model was driven more by political and economic concerns than by any humanistic desire for understanding or any recognition of a universal religiosity—the classification of people into different groups (whether religious or ethnic) being the first step toward regulating and controlling the population (Cotter and Robertson 2016, 5–6). The idea that there were a small number of "World Religions" developed directly out of the work of scholars invested in the colonial project—Max Müller (1823–1900), whose work on the Sacred Books of the East series was directly supported by the British East India Company, and Cornelius Tiele (1830–1902), who benefited from and supported the Dutch empire in less direct ways. At the colonial encounter, anything that could be made to sufficiently fit the Protestant model was considered a World Religion (Tiele, for example, presented Buddhism as basically a monotheism [1877, 3–4]), and anything else was regarded as mere primitive superstition (Chidester 1996).[1] The model they produced presented an evolutionary "tree," with each World Religion being branches growing out of a central, common religious essence. Echoing Linnaeus' contemporary organization of the natural world, it assumed a genus (and so a "natural kind," as discussed earlier), "religion," with several distinct species, World Religions. Needless to say, Christianity was always presented as the final stage of this evolution, the ultimate fruit of this tree of religions.

Essences and the Phenomenology of Religion

This colonial system of classification, and the essentialist assumptions that underpin it, became part of the foundational ethos of the emerging discipline of Religious Studies. The phenomenology of religion—an approach that dominated scholarship from the 1950s to the 1990s—centered on the claim that religions are sui generis, that is, unique unto themselves and irreducible to other categories. It was, in part, an attempt to establish a scholarly methodology to uncover these sui generis religious essences. But it was also an attempt to justify the need for a specific academic discipline dedicated to the comparative study of religions, by showing that all of these different religions were manifestations of a common phenomenon—religion—that could not be entirely grasped through sociology, philosophy, anthropology, and so on. As such, the claim that each religion has an unchanging, essential core is entangled with the claim that this core is basically the same in all religions.

The phenomenological method was established by the philosopher Edmund Husserl (1859–1938) in *Logical Investigations*, published in 1900. He argued that the essence of something was not hidden but accessible to us through our sensory perceptions, even if these were incomplete. So, he argued, when we look at a table, we never see all of the table, yet we nevertheless are able to perceive the essence of the ideal table. The German theologian Rudolf Otto (1869–1937) combined this with Friedrich Schleiermacher's (1768–1834) description of religious experience as an encounter with the Holy (or "numinous") as a "mystery both terrifying and fascinating" ("mysterium tremendum et fascinans") (1917, 13). Otto presented this encounter with the Holy as the irreducible essence of religion—accessible only through phenomenology and utterly sui generis. Through scholars like William Brede Kristensen, Chantepie de la Saussaye, and Cornelieus Tiele, phenomenology had eclipsed philology as the preeminent method in the study of religion by the time of the founding of the International Association for the History of Religions (IAHR) in 1950. The founding members of the committee Gerardus van der Leeuw, Raffaele Pettazzoni, Geo Widengren, and Claas Bleeker were all committed phenomenologists. Both van der Leeuw and Bleeker had been students of Kristensen and adopted from him a phenomenological method involving epoché (or "bracketing off" of one's personal beliefs) in order to achieve "empathetic intuition" and so scientifically perceive the essence of a given religion. Van der Leeuw's *Phänomenologie der Religion* (1933) was translated into English as *Religion in Essence and Manifestation* in 1937, and the juxtaposition of these two titles makes the essentialism of the method plain.

Through the work of these prominent scholars, and especially the appointment of Mircea Eliade at the University of Chicago in 1960, this phenomenological approach dominated Anglophone scholarship until the 1980s and continues to do so in popular discourse. Through the work of those influenced by Eliade, this phenomenological idea of all religions being at their core different expressions of the same essential experience of the sacred became a ubiquitous aspect of how religion was presented in the popular culture of the Baby Boomers as well as the ubiquitous structure of introductory courses in schools and universities. It remains so today—and indeed, the growing popularity of the "spiritual but not religious" descriptor (which relies on this distinction between particular religious institutional "manifestations" and the essence of religion which they "express") suggests that this essentialist model is as entrenched as ever.

Essentialism and the Rhetoric of Authenticity

Reducing billions of people into members of a few discrete World Religions is clearly an act of acute abstraction. Ignoring historical change and geographical diversity, it helps to create the impression of a stable set of distinct and constant things which the category religion merely disinterestedly describes. Importantly, though, in so doing we create the impression of religions as entities in their own right, independent of their members, with their own agency and existence. In his introduction to *The Norton Anthology of World Religions*, the editor Jack Miles writes of his desire to let "the six major, living, international world religions speak to readers in their own words" (2014, xli)—as though he was merely a reporter capturing oral history, rather than the person who selected not only which ones got to speak but even the specific words they used (see Cotter and Robertson 2016 for a more detailed examination of the World Religions Paradigm and its use in the classroom).

Part of the power of this idea is that it works for almost everyone with skin in the "religion" game—those invested in a particular religion, ordinary religious folk as well as the institutions themselves, and also the state which must manage them. Perhaps this is why critical scholars of religion have had such little success undermining these kinds of assumptions. The fact is that the idea that something has remained constant and unchanging over centuries or millennia has a certain rhetorical weight, which makes it hard to challenge and even more so if that essence is something that comes from some sort of divine realm.

The basis of the claim that each religion has an authentic, unchanging core is an attempt to shore up the identity of a particular religious tradition—

Christianity, Buddhism, Islam, or anything—against the evidence of historical change. In one way, it helps shore up the idea that, despite the lack of a consistent doctrine, or practice, or experience, there is nevertheless a single thing called Christianity, Buddhism, and so on, even when members of these supposed entities disagree with one another. It also helps to explain to members how it can be that the traditions of former ages can be so different, yet still be the same thing. Sure, practices evolve and theologies need to address different social contexts, but at its core, at its essence, it's still the same tradition.

But that points to another important function—an unchanging core or essence around which the externals evolve over time is a more powerful proposition than one where there is little uniting it than the name (Hobsbawm 1983 [2015], 12–14). An unchanging core is somehow outside of history, and so outside of human agency, and so is perceived as carrying much more authority than a mere human system or social construct. This is why religious institutions prefer to refer to themselves as "religious traditions"—and it's why new religions are not taken seriously and often dismissed as mere "cults."[2]

And for the individual religious spokesperson, convincing others that you have access to the *real* version of the religion can be a powerful route to authority. Authority—"the right to speak" (Hammer 2001, 37)—is frequently a subtle reinterpretation of a tradition or doctrine, yet almost always appeals to a longer tradition and often to the founder themselves. In his chapter on the Buddhist "Sacred Garden" at Lumbinī in Southern Nepal, for example, John Strong shows how every one of the twenty-plus groups with a temple, monastery, or center there claims direct connection in some way to the Buddha Śākyamuni or another pivotal figure in Buddhist history, such as the Indian Emperor Aśoka—including the site of the Sacred Garden itself (Strong 2015, 29–86).

For religious institutions too, the idea that there is some sort of theological essence or core to religions helps to authorize the sui generis nature of religion—and thus its unique importance to society. This is even more the case when the essential core is common to *all* religion, which is unsurprisingly a central claim of interfaith dialogue. Arguing that religion is a sui generis phenomenon, and that all religions reflect this common core in different ways despite external differences, helps representatives of these different traditions to work together to shore up their social capital in the face of declining institutional power and membership.

On the other hand, this argument works for detractors too. The idea that a religion is one monolithic, unchanging entity, with its own purpose, makes it so much easier to portray its adherents as mindless, or to say that *all* members of a religion are dangerous because a minority have used that religion to justify their violence or homophobia. The rhetoric of authenticity cuts both ways (Hughes 2015, xiv–xv).

Yet, as we have seen, that's all these claims ultimately are—rhetoric. And that means we can challenge them. As van Buren notes,

> Christianity has been changing since its beginning, the religion of the past constantly being adapted to the conditions of each new present. Once we see this character of Christianity, we are released from the misconceived task of trying to identify its unchanging essence. (1972, 19)

So you can just sell them the damn cake.

7

"Religion and Science Naturally Conflict"

Donovan Schaefer

In the summer of 1860, less than a year after the publication of Charles Darwin's *On the Origin of Species*, science and religion went to war. At an important public conference, a scientist named Thomas Henry Huxley challenged the Bishop of Oxford, Samuel Wilberforce, about the new evolutionary biology. In a hot room in front of about 700 people, they clashed over the proper place of science and religion in society. (If you go to the Museum of Natural History in Oxford today, you can see a monument out front commemorating the event [Figure 7.1].)

It might seem strange to say that science and religion went to war just 150 years ago. Many people (especially in the United States in the twenty-first century) believe that science and religion have always been at war and probably always will be—at least until one of them wins. But the truth is that even though the exact starting point of the hostilities between science and religion is hard to pin down, what historians call the *conflict thesis*—the idea that religion and science naturally conflict—seems to have been created in the Anglo-American world in the nineteenth century. (This chapter will focus almost entirely on this Anglo-American context of science. Interestingly, the conflict thesis looks very different from the perspective of other people, places, and religious traditions, as books like *Science and Religion around the World* have shown.)

This chapter will consider the conflict thesis in history. It will show that the claim that science and religion always clash is not supported by historical evidence. In the first part, we'll look at why most people before the nineteenth

FIGURE 7.1 *Monument commemorating the debate between Huxley and Wilberforce at the Oxford Museum of Natural History.*

century believed science and religion were in harmony. In the second part, we'll home in on one of the most famous examples of (what seems like) science-religion conflict: the trials of Galileo Galilei in the seventeenth century. Throughout, we will see that the conflict thesis really rests on a particularly narrow way of understanding "science" and "religion" as easy to extract from their historical, political, and cultural contexts. In fact, as we'll see, science and religion are complicated categories, with meanings that change over time and are often hard to extricate from other things that are happening around them. This means the conflict thesis is wrong, but so is the claim made by some other thinkers that "true science" and "true religion" don't conflict.

From Collaboration to Conflict

What changed in the nineteenth century? Up until the early nineteenth century, it was almost always the case that when science and religion came together, they did so in a spirit of cooperation rather than competition. The oldest English-language universities—Oxford and Cambridge—began as religious institutions, collections of religious "halls" or miniature monasteries where men who were in religious orders gathered with a mission of study and education. This is why most of the constituent colleges of Cambridge and Oxford, founded in the Middle Ages, are named after Christian saints. Oxford alone has two colleges named after St. Mary.

In the United States, about a dozen institutions of higher learning appeared between colonization and the American revolution. These institutions, too, were usually religious in character. We can see this in their mottos:

Princeton University—*Dei Sub Numine Viget* ("Under the light of God she flourishes")

Brown University—*In Deo Speramus* ("In God we hope")

Columbia University—*In lumine Tuo videbimus lumen* ("In Thy light shall we see light," from Psalm 36)

Oxford and Cambridge also have religious mottos, reflecting their background as primarily Christian places.

Oxford University—*Dominus illuminatio mea* ("The Lord is my light")

Cambridge University—*Hinc lucem et pocula sacra* ("From here [we derive] light and sacred draughts")

In the UK, it was a requirement that all fellows and professors at Oxford and Cambridge take holy orders—that is, become ordained as priests—right up until the late nineteenth century. In the late 1600s, Isaac Newton famously refused to do this, not because he rejected religion but because he rejected the doctrine of the Trinity in Christian theology. (His home college at Cambridge—coincidentally named Trinity College—allowed him to waive this requirement. Wise choice!)

Although many modern universities have now detached themselves from the religious institutions that founded them, the original way universities came into being—through church sponsorship—can still be seen in Catholic universities like Georgetown, Notre Dame, and Villanova. We might now think of science and religion as separate things, but it's important to remember that the first foundations dedicated to creating scientific knowledge were religious institutions, and most of the first people we would now think of as scientists in the English-speaking world were members of holy orders.

The connection goes even deeper, though. This is because much of the research that was done at the beginning of what we now think of as the scientific revolution in the sixteenth and seventeenth centuries was used to *strengthen religious claims*. The seventeenth-century astronomer Johannes Kepler, for instance, saw the solar system as a metaphor for the Christian Trinity, in which the Father was the sun, the Son was the stars or periphery, and the Holy Spirit was the relationship connecting them all together (Rubenstein 2014, 112). Isaac Newton closed his *Principia Mathematica* with a famous "Scholium" or commentary, in which he wrote "This most beautiful system of the sun, planets, and comets, could only proceed from the counsel and dominion of an intelligent and powerful Being" (Newton 1846).

Newton also worked closely with the master of his home institution—Trinity College, Cambridge—to help him write lectures that proved the truth of Christianity against the claims of Muslims, Jews, and atheists. This was an early example of what is called "natural theology," which means *using the findings of science to prove the existence of God*. The most prominent Christian natural theologian was also from Trinity College, but he wrote almost a century after Newton died. His name was William Paley, and his book *Natural Theology*, published in 1802, is one of the best illustrations of what we're talking about. His book is filled with up-to-date scientific diagrams showing the structure of the eye, muscles, and the skeleton. Why? He argued that the *complexity* of all these structures *proved* the existence of an intelligent superbeing who had created everything. How could the intricate mechanisms of the eye have occurred by accident?

But within half a century, the tide had turned. More and more, science and religion were seen not only as separate but at odds. Theories of evolution had a lot to do with this. It's important to remember that even though today we most strongly associate evolution with Charles Darwin (and his was certainly the first theory of evolution that was truly successful in the arena of science), there were a number of prominent evolutionists before him. Fifteen years before Darwin's *Origin* was published, for instance, another book proposed the evolution of all life on earth. Called *Vestiges of the Natural History of Creation*, it was published anonymously but became an international bestseller. It drew on fields like geology and archaeology as well as what we would now think of as biology.

Critics of these books believed that they were doing a new kind of science that was harmful to religion. There were several overlapping issues. For one thing, it seemed that these new kinds of science were highlighting the messiness of nature, rather than the harmony of nature. Archaeological research was turning up fossils and imprints of species that no longer seemed to exist. Could species go extinct? But how could that be possible in the perfect world created by God? For another thing, these new sciences seemed to contradict some of the stories found within scripture. Theories of evolution that suggested humans emerged from earlier animal organisms contrasted sharply with the stories of special creation found in Genesis. And moreover, these new sciences challenged the hierarchy of society, in which every stratum of society from the pauper to the emperor was put there by divine law. Paley was writing, in part, in reaction to the French Revolution of

1789, which had seen the violent destruction of the French aristocracy. Could these new sciences be to blame?

In the latter half of the nineteenth century, more and more people believed science and religion were splitting apart. Some were alarmed by this. One of Darwin's old teachers wrote in a letter to a friend that Darwin's *Origin*

> repudiates all reasoning from final causes; and seems to shut the door upon any view (however feeble) of the God of Nature as manifested in His works. From first to last it is a dish of rank materialism cleverly cooked and served up. . . . It is a system embracing all living nature, vegetable and animal; yet contradicting-point blank-the vast treasury of facts that [God] has, during the past two or three thousand years, revealed to our senses. And why is this done? For no other solid reason, I am sure, except to make us independent of a Creator. (Sedgwick, Clark, and Hughes 1890, 360)

But others celebrated it. Thomas Henry Huxley wrote a gleeful review of *Origin*, clearly delighted that it could be used as a weapon against religious belief. "Extinguished theologians," he said, "lie about the cradle of every science as the strangled snakes beside that of Hercules; and history records that whenever science and orthodoxy have been fairly opposed, the latter has been forced to retire from the lists, bleeding and crushed if not annihilated; scotched, if not slain" (Huxley 1896, 52).

More and more, people began to talk about science and religion as being in conflict. In the room when Huxley debated the Bishop of Oxford in 1860 was a professor of chemistry from New York University, John William Draper. Draper would eventually publish the book *History of the Conflict between Religion and Science*, which argued that rather than being allies, science and religion are opposed. The "conflict thesis" takes its name from this title. Other books like *A History of the Warfare of Science with Theology in Christendom* by Andrew Dickson White (the founder of Cornell University) followed. At the same time, thinkers like Karl Marx and Auguste Comte suggested that religion was in a state of decline and would gradually disappear as society advanced, what we now call the "secularization thesis."

In the twentieth century, this picture of science and religion in conflict gained even more force during the Scopes Trial of 1925. In the Scopes Trial, a law advanced by Christian fundamentalists forbidding the teaching of anything contradicting the biblical Book of Genesis was used to prosecute a science teacher, John T. Scopes. The trial became a media circus, brought into public awareness through newspapers and radio broadcasts. Thirty years later, the events of the Scopes Trial were turned into a play and later a movie, *Inherit the Wind*. *Inherit the Wind* took out key aspects of the story—like the fact that Scopes volunteered to be prosecuted to help test the constitutionality of the law. This made the science-religion conflict angle seem even sharper than it was.

Throughout the first half of the twentieth century, critics of science became even more alarmed by new ideas coming from the field of psychology. Psychology, it seemed to them, was increasingly focusing on how human beings were determined by their circumstances, whether this was the "conditioning" processes suggested by behaviorism or the "unconscious" influences explored by Sigmund Freud's school of psychoanalysis. Christian commentators like Reinhold Niebuhr saw these new trends as incompatible with Christian morality and Christian ideas about salvation (Jewett 2020). Over the course of the twentieth century, some religious critics of science continued to develop these ideas, becoming especially wary of what they perceived as the expansion of a scientific worldview (sometimes called "scientism" or "secularism") and the displacement of the authority of traditional religion.

Meanwhile, from the other side, critics of religion's encroachment into the domain of science pointed to the continuing battles around the teaching of evolution in schools. Laws like the one in Tennessee that forbid teaching evolution in public high schools were on the books in many states until 1968, when a schoolteacher named Susan Epperson became the center of a case in Arkansas. This case went all the way to the Supreme Court, which struck down the laws as unconstitutional. The battlefield then shifted to "equal time" laws, which legislated that evolutionary biology and biblical creation stories must be given equivalent platforms in classrooms. These, too, were ruled unconstitutional in 1987. Some Christian activists have since then insisted on the need to teach theories like "intelligent design" in biology classes, in spite of a lack of scientific evidence.

The Galileo Affair

So far we've looked at the history of how we came to *see* science and religion as being in conflict—a view that would have seemed strange just 200 years ago. And we're starting to get a feel for just how *complicated* situations of what looks like science-religion conflict actually are. They pull in not just science and religion but political and cultural contests over authority and power. We can get an even better picture of just how complicated these issues actually are by zooming in on a case study, what historians call the "Galileo affair."

Draper's *History of the Conflict between Science and Religion* popularized the relatively new conflict thesis. One of his innovations was to look more closely at the persecution of the Italian astronomer Galileo Galilei in the seventeenth century. Even though this event had taken place over 200 years earlier, the nineteenth century saw a new interest in the Galileo affair. Documents related to the trial came to light smack dab in the middle of the controversies surrounding Darwin in the late nineteenth century, for instance. Draper identified it as one of the five "great conflicts" between science and religion. We didn't discuss the Galileo affair in the previous section, but it's so important for understanding what the conflict thesis gets wrong that it's worth spending the rest of this chapter on it. As with the Scopes Trial, the basic contours of the Galileo affair are well known, but vital details are often overlooked.

Galileo Galilei was a natural philosopher born in the city of Pisa (part of the Duchy of Florence) in 1564. (We call him a natural philosopher rather than a "scientist" because the word "scientist" wasn't used until the nineteenth century, when it was invented by William Whewell, a mentor of Charles Darwin at Trinity College.) He studied at the University of Pisa and became interested in topics like astronomy and physics. In 1609, Galileo heard a story about a new device that had been built in the Netherlands—a tube containing glass lenses and mirrors that could make distant objects appear as if they were much closer. Galileo quickly figured out how to build his own telescope. He gave the designs to the Doge of Venice, who was so impressed by its potential military applications that he gave Galileo a university appointment for life. Galileo then used his telescope to begin looking at the skies.

Galileo gave a demonstration of his telescope at the University of Padua, showing off some of the discoveries he had made, things like mountains and craters on Earth's moon, four of the moons of Jupiter, and the phases of Venus. (Remember that Venus, like Earth's moon and all other objects in our solar system, waxes and wanes in phases according to its position between us and the sun, though only the moon's phases can be seen with the naked eye.) But two professors at the demonstration refused to look through the telescope. They didn't want to see what he had to show them. Were they Catholic priests? Or bishops? Or even theologians? In fact, both were professors of philosophy.

Why did the philosophy professors refuse to look through the telescope? And what was it about mountains on the moon that bothered them in the first place? To understand this, we need to consider the intellectual background of how Catholic Christians understood the solar system in Galileo's time. Catholic scholarship in this era was dominated by the thought of an earlier figure, St. Thomas Aquinas, who had lived and died in the thirteenth century. Aquinas' main contribution was connecting Christian theology with the work of the (pre-Christian) Greek philosopher Aristotle, who was already very popular among Muslim theologians and philosophers of the time. One of the philosophers who refused to look through Galileo's telescope was Cesare Cremonini, a "Professor of Aristotelian Philosophy" at the university.

Aristotle and many other ancient thinkers had a "geocentric" view of the solar system. This meant Earth was at the center, with the sun, moon, and other planets orbiting us. But they also had a *very* different view of what those celestial bodies were. Specifically, they thought that the sun, moon, and planets were not material things at all. They were more like philosophical abstractions that existed in a realm of perfect beings above us. They were visible from our place—which was the corrupt realm of material things—but they were a fundamentally different kind of entity. They were, these philosophers believed, perfect spheres, and they moved in perfect, mathematically predictable circular orbits.

Galileo's discoveries with his telescope sharply contradicted this view of the cosmos. Jupiter's moons, for instance, messed up the neat layers of concentric orbits that the philosophers expected. The phases of Venus were strange, too, because they suggested that Venus was orbiting the sun rather than Earth. This is what we now call the "heliocentric" view—the sun is at the center of the solar system. The astronomer Nicolaus Copernicus had predicted that Venus and other planets would have phases like the moon in his book advocating heliocentrism published in Poland seventy years previous. But just as confusing were the mountains on the moon. How could the moon—a perfect sphere—have craters and mountains like an ordinary rock? It seems obvious to us now, but all these ideas made philosophers of the time extremely uncomfortable. Galileo found this silly. He later wrote:

> These doctors of philosophy never concede the moon to be less polished than a mirror; they want it to be more so, if that can be imagined, for they deem that only perfect shapes can suit perfect bodies. Hence the sphericity of the heavenly globes must be absolute. (in Drake 2001, 80)

Before we get into what happened next, we need to fill in two other aspects of the background of this situation: the *religious* backdrop and the *political* backdrop.

The religious backdrop is very important. In 1517, the Catholic monk Martin Luther launched a sharp challenge to the teachings of the Catholic Church, triggering the events we now call the Protestant Reformation. Most of Europe, up until this time, was affiliated with the Catholic Church. But after the Reformation, several areas (especially those far away from the Catholic power base in Rome) veered away from Catholicism and adopted various forms of Protestantism.

Although there had already been one major schism in Christianity, 500 years earlier, the shock of the Reformation was traumatic for the Catholic Church. Not only that, the Reformation led to a number of extremely violent wars, which continued to reverberate for centuries after 1517. From 1618 to 1648, for instance, the "Thirty Years War" drew in a number of different political factions, often (though not always) divided on religious lines. This war killed as much as one-third of the population of the German states where most of it was fought. (Imagine a war today that killed one-third of the population of a country—that would mean over 100 million people in the United States.) These theological and religious questions were not abstractions in this time. They had real political consequences—and often violent ones.

That brings us to the political backdrop. The Italian peninsula in Galileo's time was not "Italy." It was a grab bag of different states. This included a special kind of state: the Papal States. The Papal States (also known as the "State of the Church") were ruled by the pope just as a monarch would rule their domain—passing laws, collecting taxes, mobilizing armies, and invading territory. This might seem strange to us now, since we don't think of the church as having an "earthly" power base. But during this time, it was understood that the Catholic Church was both a church and a state. Even when they weren't physically fighting each other, the states of the Italian peninsula (including the Papal States) were in a constant struggle for influence and control, using alliances, diplomacy, espionage, and economic power to advance their interests.

What all this underlines is that Galileo was playing a high-stakes game. He knew this and had his own strategies and tactics. His patrons in the Grand Duchy of Tuscany, the ruthless Medici family, had opened doors in his career. He repaid their help by naming the moons of Jupiter "the Medicean stars." When controversy over his work ignited, Galileo appealed directly to the Grand Duchess Christina (mother of Cosimo II de' Medici) for help, writing a famous letter that was actually published twenty years later. Galileo in this missive wrapped himself in piety, insisting he was not doing anything that violated Catholic teaching, even citing earlier Catholic thinkers like St. Augustine to defend his position. He insisted that he was the true Catholic and that his enemies were trying to warp the intellectual tradition of the church. He quoted a Catholic cardinal who said "the intention of the Holy Ghost is to teach us how one goes to heaven, not how heaven goes."

But as good as Galileo was at playing this game, his opponents were better. Philosophers disturbed by his ideas formed an alliance with some powerful priests. They were determined to bring him down. This group managed to persuade the Medicis that Galileo was radioactive and that he would weaken their standing with the Catholic Church. Galileo became a political liability, and the Medicis withdrew their protection. This opened the door for the philosophical conflict to become a religious one. In 1616, Galileo was punished by the church authorities and his works were banned. Other books that had been allowed for decades—like Copernicus' 1543 *On the Revolutions* of the Heavenly Spheres—were also banned at this time. Galileo received contradictory advice about his future. Privately, he was told by a friend—a high-ranking cardinal—that he could *discuss* heliocentrism as long as he did not *defend* it. But others in the church believed that he was not allowed to *even talk* about heliocentrism going forward.

This confusion set the stage for what happened next. In 1632, Galileo published a new major book, *Dialogue of the Two Chief World Systems*, which staged a conversation between a defender of heliocentrism and a defender of geocentrism. Galileo believed that because the book was a "dialogue" rather than a statement of his position, he was being faithful to the earlier restrictions that had been placed on him. (And he dedicated the book to Grand Duke Ferdinando II de Medici to buy himself some extra insurance.) But the church saw things differently. He was put on trial and ordered to explain himself. Galileo brought receipts. He had a letter from his friend the cardinal—written seventeen years before—proving that he was allowed to talk about heliocentrism (so long as he didn't defend it). But by this point, the church was dug in. To save face, they had to convict him of something. The result was that Galileo was forbidden to publish again and sentenced to a life of house arrest. This conviction was so upsetting to some of the cardinals adjudicating the case that three of the ten members of the committee refused to sign the sentence. Galileo spent the rest of his life at his Tuscan villa and died a decade later.

Does the Galileo affair prove that science and religion naturally conflict? As we've seen just from this brief overview, the situation was much more complicated than that. On the one hand, there's the undeniable fact that Galileo was punished by the Catholic hierarchy. But the conflict began outside the church, in a philosophical debate about the nature of the moon and the planets. It was amplified by the entanglement of the church with complicated court politics—the deadly serious cloak-and-dagger business we associate with the Medicis—as well as a political backdrop in which questions about doctrine turned into spectacles where institutions like the Catholic Church had to project an image of strength and resolve.

Galileo, for his part, never saw what he was doing as irreligious, and mustered religious arguments to defend both his method and his conclusions. And he believed, right to the end of his life, that he had been victimized not by the church, but by a few vindictive men who had manipulated the tools of the church to attack him. Before Galileo's publication of his discoveries, a number of Catholics were seriously interested in the heliocentric worldview, including Copernicus himself and a number of Jesuits. The historian John Hedley Brooke talks about how religious institutions outside Italy were much more accepting of heliocentrism. He mentions the English Copernican John Wilkins, who not only was the master of Trinity College but was eventually appointed to a special role preaching to the king (Brooke 1991, 144). By the end of the seventeenth century—within half a century of Galileo's death—Newton and Kepler had established heliocentrism as the dominant scientific model of the solar system in both Catholic and Protestant countries in Europe.

The Thirty Years War happening at the same time is a good analogy here. Although it is considered part of the European Wars of Religion kicked off by the Protestant Reformation, it quickly mutated into something much more complex: conflict between competing dynasties (the Habsburgs and the Bourbons), territorial clashes, and jockeying for influence among the member states of the Holy Roman Empire. By the end, Catholics were fighting Catholics. Along the same lines, Brooke urges us to recall that the Galileo affair was an isolated incident, powerfully defined by political and historical circumstances and very much out of character with how the Catholic Church typically transacted with science (Brooke 1991, 146).

Conclusion: Looking Again at "Science" and "Religion"

This history is important. It proves that we need to step back from the conflict thesis that says science and religion are always at war. In fact, the idea that science and religion are at war is relatively recent. But it also shows that the concepts "science" and "religion" are a lot harder to nail down than we might expect. Is the Aristotelian understanding of the moon and the planets as perfect spheres a "religious" or a "scientific" idea? We may well think that we know what we mean by the words "science" and "religion." But ultimately, both of these things are so entangled with philosophy, history, culture, and politics that it can be hard to tell where one ends and another begins.

Draper's own book is a good example of this. Although Draper's title plays up the contrast between science and religion, it's clear that his real concern is with the Catholic Church. His examples of the five "great conflicts" between science and religion include not only the Galileo affair but the Protestant Reformation, medieval debates over the nature of the soul, and even the birth of Islam, which he calls the "First or Southern Reformation"—none of which we consider as being about "science" as we understand it now. His conclusion was that the Catholic Church can't ever work with science, but "a reconciliation of the Reformation with Science is not only possible, but would easily take place" (Draper 2009, 363). But in the twentieth century, the Catholic Church became one of the main Christian denominations embracing the theory of evolution, while Protestant fundamentalists opposed it. So

Draper's enemy doesn't seem to be "religion," in general, but a particular form of religion in a particular time and place.

White's book on the "warfare" between science and religion also does not condemn religion as such, but rather "dogmatic theology." "My conviction," he states, "is that Science, though it has evidently conquered Dogmatic Theology based on biblical texts and ancient modes of thought, will go hand in hand with Religion" (White 2009, xii). So we need to be very clear about what religion and science actually *are* for these authors. Only by understanding how these words are being used in a particular time and place can we understand what it means to talk about them as being in collaboration or in conflict.

In the end, it's important to disentangle different *versions* of the conflict thesis. The claim "religion and science naturally conflict" is really an example of what we might call the *strong* conflict thesis, which says that religion and science are fundamentally different *kinds* of things, and the kinds of things they are will always clash. Religion and science can't occupy the same space at the same time. As we've seen, this just isn't true. What gets called "religion" and what gets called "science" have cooperated many times throughout history. Arguably, science emerged out of religious institutions. Even Galileo thought what he was doing was fully compatible with religion. So the strong conflict thesis falls apart.

On the other hand, sometimes "religion" and "science" really do have disagreements—even if those disagreements are hard to disentangle from political, historical, and personal conflict. This means we need to be equally careful about statements like "true science and true religion never conflict." Galileo's claim that religion teaches us how to get to heaven and science teaches us how the heavens go has been echoed by modern thinkers, like the Harvard paleontologist Stephen Jay Gould. The problem with this view is that it assumes that there really is such a thing as "true science" or "true religion" that can be separated out from historical context. But as we've seen, there is no pure religion and no pure science. That means we need to study their interactions up close, rather than assuming that one rule will explain their relationship in all times and places.

8

"Conservative Religions Oppress Women (While Liberal Religions Don't)"

Leslie Dorrough Smith

In September 2021, an Atlanta newspaper ran a single-frame political cartoon entitled "Sisterhood." In it, two women in burqas (in a stereotypical desert setting that most Americans would likely read as the Middle East) are featured together. The only text in the cartoon is one telling the other to "Pray for Texas Women. . . " (Lukovich 2021). This was not the only editorial cartoon to play upon this theme. In the same week, a Maryland newspaper ran a very similar piece where two women, also in full-body coverings are speaking. One, from Afghanistan, asks the other if she's from that country, too; the other responds, "No . . . Texas" (Stahler 2021).

The stories behind these cartoons involve a series of political events that, while different, coalesced at about the same time. In September 2021, the state of Texas enacted a law that effectively banned abortion statewide, sending shockwaves across the country. Although the law doesn't officially prohibit abortions outright, it makes the time that a woman can acquire the procedure so short that most women do not even know they are pregnant. Since the overturning of *Roe v. Wade* in June 2022, several other states have followed suit with similar laws. The Texas law was thus very emotionally evocative because it provided the first indication of impending abortion restrictions in light of a more conservative era in the US Supreme Court. Texas has long been known as a "red state," and while it is quite large and politically diverse in many ways, conservative Christians are often influential in political contests.

The second event, which roughly coincided with the Texas abortion policy, was the United States' withdrawal of troops from Afghanistan after a twenty-year military presence. The war in Afghanistan was one of America's longest wars, beginning under the leadership of President George W. Bush shortly after 9/11, and initiated in the name of stopping various groups of Muslim radicals (namely, Al Qaeda and the Taliban) responsible for that and other acts of global terrorism. Those of us who witnessed the beginning of this war firsthand may remember that one of the most compelling symbols used to rally the American public's support for the invasion were images of Afghan women wearing burqas. To the Bush administration, invading Afghanistan was seen as not just retaliation in the name of the United States but saving these women from what had to be miserable lives thanks to the chains of radical Islam. When the Taliban swiftly took over the country upon the 2021 American withdrawal, American news agencies once again appealed to the plight of Afghan women as a sign of the Taliban's penchant for cultural degradation.

It's not hard to see, then, that for these political commentators (and many others, as well), both the women of Texas and Afghanistan were oppressed entities at the mercy of conservative religion (with the burqa, acting as a stand-in for Islam, serving as its major symbol). The notion that conservative religions oppress women and that liberal ones do not is so widely embraced in many circles that it may seem common sense. One reason for these assumptions is that there appears to be substantial data to back them. Many conservative branches of religious traditions often openly tout their belief in a gendered relationship often called "complementarianism." While the word has been used widely to describe conservative Christian gender norms, the concept is found globally: men and women have inherently different, divinely designed natures and thus must lead different roles in life; when paired together, the strengths of one complement the strengths of the other (and thus the name).

Critics of complementarianism point to several areas to refute it. First off, gender norms around the world can vary wildly, which shows that these roles are not how humans are "naturally" designed. But, they also note, the fact that men are always named leaders in such systems and women followers seems rather convenient for the men, and thus is simply a sign of a sexist hierarchy—of an "abuse" of religion that more progressive groups long ago rejected. For the liberal or progressive religious groups that offer such critiques, giving full status, rights, and power to women (and, often, the LGBTQ community) is clearly the only moral choice.

But are things this simple? The aim of this chapter is to dissect the claim that conservative religions oppress women while liberal ones don't. While it may be generally true that groups that identify as conservative tend to be more restrictive of women than other types of groups, this observation is simple only on the surface. First, we have to consider what we mean by conservative and liberal, as well as what we mean by oppression. Conversations about oppression often lead to parallel discussions about choice: that is, if a woman freely chooses to be part of a religious group that limits her agency and power, then is she really oppressed at all? After looking at how scholars have dealt with these issues, we'll examine further how this stereotype operates in real life. What I hope to provide here is a series of questions and further considerations that demonstrate the nuance and complexity behind this very popular claim.

The Issues behind the Stereotypes

The idea that certain forms of traditional or conservative religion oppress women has been around for as long as people have recorded their interactions with other cultures and their religious practices, as we will shortly discuss. But to consider the full significance of such claims in both the past and the present, we need to think about not only why certain groups are described as perpetuating gender oppression but also what the terms "conservative" and "liberal" have meant in these contexts. While these terms take on specific meanings when applied to political systems (and we need to separate them from their political context, to some degree, in this chapter), these words have also been used to signify general attitudes toward social order and social change.

As it is stereotypically described, conservatism is often associated with traditionalism and a desire to restore a certain idealization of the past. Conservative movements are often less concerned about recognizing a diversity of perspectives if those views challenge the vision of a more traditional type of social order. It is true that these traditional arrangements have, historically, favored men, and particularly, normatively gendered, straight men who represent the racially dominant group. This is why, for instance, many conservative religions tend to favor ideas of heterosexual male leadership or superiority and female subservience or inferiority.

On the flip side, the stereotype about liberal movements is that they are more open to diversity, novelty, and multiple perspectives. They are often associated with the rejection of older forms of authority and social organization in the name of creating a more equitable society. Many argue that these ideas are reflected in more progressive religious groups' willingness to do things like ordain women as religious leaders, break down gender divisions and norms, and accept and support the LGBTQ community.

Clearly, then, the idea that conservative religions oppress women while liberal ones don't is rooted in certain ideas about authority and social organization and, to some degree, these distinctions are true. Yet while these labels hold some explanatory usefulness, we have to recognize that, like all categories, they can be moving targets. This is not just because attitudes about topics like traditionalism, the past, diversity, and equity are different from one culture and one time to another; it is also because, when these ideas are put into action, they are used widely by many different groups of people, which dismantles the idea that these words describe two distinct camps. In fact, the ideas behind the labels "conservative" and "liberal" might be best understood as tools that various people and groups can use for a variety of purposes (Dorrough Smith 2019, 9).

One very clear example of this occurred in the midst of the COVID-19 pandemic. The American conservative media pundit Tucker Carlson, who has generally been a critic of the COVID-19 vaccine, responded to those entities mandating it with the commonly used liberal abortion rights phrase, "our body, our choice" (Villareal 2021). While Carlson certainly understood the irony of what he was saying, he was endorsing a position associated with those who call themselves conservatives by using a slogan associated with those who call themselves liberals. Why did he use it? The answer is that it served his purposes: it was meant to chastise liberals for what he considered hypocrisy at the same time that it endorsed his particular position. In this sense, a person or group that identifies as conservative may, at times, use liberal ideas or types of speech depending on the situation; the same is true of a person or group that identifies as liberal. Consider that while the stereotype indicates that conservative groups are the ones that wish to restore a particular vision of the past, it is absolutely the case that liberal groups also make appeals to the past when doing so suits their social goals. There is not a clear line between these groups because these two positions are used as social persuasion strategies. They are not, in other words, only ideals.

So far, then, we've established that the labels "liberal" and "conservative" don't necessarily describe distinct groups, nor do the ideas themselves have firm boundaries. Again, we can think of them, instead, as labels used by many different types of people to meet their diverse goals. But if we are to understand the main claim here—that conservative religions oppress women while liberal ones don't—we must press this issue further to think about the degree to which a culture tolerates oppression against certain members of its population, and whether it even recognizes these arrangements as oppressive.

The scholar Marilyn Frye, in her famous essay simply entitled "Oppression," noted that oppression is a state where a person's agency and choice is constrained on all sides, leading to an endless series of double binds. As an example, Frye describes the classic case of women who are called "prudes" if they aren't sexually forthcoming with men, but "sluts" if they are (Frye 1983, 3). Outsiders may not be able to see all of the sources of constraint because they are accustomed to them—again, they take them for granted—but being pressed into a mold not of your own making is the central feature of oppression (1983, 2).

If oppression is not always immediately visible to outsiders, Frye is also quick to clarify that one's feelings about one's experiences are also not necessarily indicative of whether one is oppressed. Not everyone can claim to be oppressed just because they don't like something; this distinction, Frye argues, constitutes the difference between discomfort and oppression. Discomfort can be an unpleasant or even deeply painful experience, but one that doesn't fundamentally harm the overall power that one has to respond to a situation or in the world, more generally (1983, 11). On the flip side, if bad feelings aren't necessarily a sign of oppression, good feelings aren't necessarily a sign of its absence; we can't regard women as unoppressed just because they aren't miserable. Oppression is not a feeling, but a calculus of power—the degree to which one can actually control the terms of one's life (1983, 7ff).

Frye's claims have evoked controversial arguments over whether it is possible for people to choose to be in oppressive circumstances. If one chooses to be in those groups, isn't that a sign of agency (i.e., of nonoppression)? On the other hand, some argue, if one is simply unaware that there are other choices, or one cannot reasonably pursue other options, constraint may feel like freedom if you're being rewarded for conforming, and that is precisely why oppressive circumstances may be tolerated by many for so long. This perspective is an outgrowth of the Marxist false-consciousness concept that some people will do things that are not in their own best interest because their view of reality has been twisted by others who benefit from this misconception.

Frye's larger point is that entire cultures can normalize various types of oppression without recognizing it as such, and, for our purposes, it is important to acknowledge that religion is one tool used in this normalization process. This is because most religious groups function like a mirror, reflecting and supporting their larger culture's norms and interests. This means that a sexist culture will generally produce sexist religious groups, while a racist culture will generally produce racist religious groups, and so on. This observation is a general summary of scholar Pierre Bourdieu's concept of habitus, which refers to the processes by which cultures naturalize oppression. In many cases, whatever is regarded as natural by a culture will generally be seen as moral by the general population, at least to some degree, and thus will become a seemingly self-evident social standard. In other words, if they become routine, bias and prejudice may be seen as simply "the way things are" and not of any particular moral concern because they are simply taken for granted.

Observations like this are important for us in thinking about whether conservative religious groups are more likely to oppress women (while liberal groups are not), for if a certain degree of gender inequality is "baked in" to a culture, so to speak, then it may be the case that most groups in a culture participate in this, even if unconsciously so. This is significant for the stereotype in question because it means that oppression is not the exclusive domain of conservative groups alone. If we can acknowledge, then, that religion is a type of authority one job of which is to reinforce preexisting cultural ideas, then this may help us further unpack the role that religions play in perpetuating gendered oppression.

Up to this point, it may feel like we've asked more questions than delivered answers, but here's what we've established: while conservative and liberal identities may somewhat correlate with the number and type of opportunities granted to women, both identities are products of their cultures (and the gendered limitations built into them). In this sense, neither identity is solid or stable but is used in shifting ways to accommodate the social needs and interests of the group in question. We've also established that oppression is a complex issue involving the degree to which one has agency in the world, and not just how one feels about one's conditions. There's not much doubt that many conservative religious groups have limited women's power compared to men, and using Frye's definition, it is fair to call that oppression. But it is also not exactly clear that what more liberal groups offer is always "liberation," either.

How Scholars Have Contributed to/ Challenged This Stereotype

Scholars of many fields have had a complicated relationship with the notion that conservative religions oppress, while liberal ones don't. In response, there have been two dominant approaches (very generally): one approach embraces this idea, often within the context of promoting more liberal religious forms as consistent with liberal democratic values. The other approach examines how this idea has been used to cause harm, often by spreading Western imperialism.

As far as the first approach is concerned, we can trace these attitudes to a number of pro-diversity movements starting as early as the mid-twentieth century in the United States with the civil rights movements, but gaining scholarly steam by the 1980s. These movements and scholars understood pluralism, diversity, and equity as values that were beneficial, and the rigidity and traditionalism often associated with more conservative movements as antiquated and hurtful. Many such scholars advocated for interfaith cooperation and activism that tended to use liberal Protestant Christian ideals (which tend to consider religion as something personal, private, peace-loving, and socially liberal) as the norm for proper religious practice. This became a particularly urgent distinction to make for many in the United States after the 9/11 attacks when anti-Muslim violence broke out across the country. In response, virtually every mainstream media organization attempted to distinguish between "good Muslims" and "bad Muslims."

Perhaps the epitome of this scholarly perspective was the 2002 publication of *A New Religious America: How a "Christian Country" Has Become the World's Most Religiously Diverse Nation*, by scholar Diana Eck, who was particularly influential in promoting the idea that the ideal society would promote a "symphony" of religious groups working together rather than subjecting minority groups to a process of forced assimilation (Eck 2001, 56). Eck's work was one sign of a general acknowledgment by many scholars that religious groups comfortable with this symphony model (many of whom we could call "liberal") were beneficial to American culture, and those who were not (who many would call "conservative") were not.

Yet not everyone who embraced this first approach agreed on what constituted "good religion." Regarding gender, the issue for many was whether it was possible to eradicate sexism from a religious system that had been developed in a sexist context. Many feminist scholars of religion in the 1970s–1990s believed it was possible to overcome sexism within established patriarchal traditions so long as one advocated for new readings of religious texts, promoted new interpretations of rituals and ethics, and otherwise challenged highly entrenched, patriarchal models. But other feminist scholars rejected the idea that any religion rooted in patriarchal structures could be salvaged at all. They called for a complete rejection of such traditions and/or the embrace of new religions that were woman-centered (often forms of paganism) and thus supposedly free of the sexism that had for so long characterized many more mainstream religious groups.

The second approach in recent scholarship has studied the impact of Western forces and ideals on peoples of other countries and has examined how more traditional/conservative religious practices of these regions have been used as a justification for foreign invasion, whether physical or cultural. For instance, historian Nicholas Dirks notes that this was a common theme among many nineteenth-century British observers who wrote about various Indian religious forms during the British colonization of India. Observing the custom of *sati*, or widow-burning (whereupon a widowed woman immolates herself on her dead husband's funeral pyre), many British observers concluded not just that the act was problematic but that the British invasion of India was warranted because they needed to "civilize" the Indian people (Dirks 2001,

152). As we will shortly discuss, members of the global feminist movement have also cautioned scholars and activists alike that while there may sometimes be ethical grounds for providing aid to women in other countries who live in oppressive situations bolstered by religion, this rationale has also been one of the dominant guises ("liberation") under which Western imperialism has taken place.

Related to this, another group of scholars (many of them feminist women) have specifically questioned the ways in which false-consciousness arguments have been used to portray many of the world's religious women as helpless, often in order to justify ethnocentrism and/or to perpetuate stereotypes that make more liberal cultures and religions appear superior. Most of these scholars believe that the characterization of conservative religious women as mindlessly brainwashed is simply inaccurate. While many women in conservative religious groups would like aspects of their life circumstances to change, they note, this does not negate the fact that they value their religious identities and have made conscious decisions to remain committed to such groups. Feminist scholars like Chandra Talpade Mohanty, Saba Mahmood, and Lila Abu-Lughod, who have studied women from across Southeast Asia, the Middle East, and North Africa (among others), have further shown that Western commentators have been eager to try to "save" foreign women from their conservative religions (often, Islam and Hinduism) by war, colonialism, forced conversions, and imperialist attitudes that promote a very damaging type of cultural condescension. (Much of what these scholars have written is applicable to this discussion; specifically, though, see Mohanty 2003; Mahmood 2011; and Abu-Lughod 2015).

Importantly, none of these scholars have argued that these women's situations were ideal, free of oppression, nor that they had as much power as the men around them. Much of their critique, rather, was in regard to the very dichotomous, one-dimensional way that scholars and other commentators were characterizing such women, their religious motivations, and their cultures more generally without asking whether these same dynamics were occurring in Western and Christian cultures. The result, they argue, is the promotion of white Western saviors who can make their own religions and cultures appear superior and rational in contrast, all while conveniently overlooking the ways that religions closer to home are also subjecting women to numerous types of constraints. Put differently, while observers have recognized the ways that conservative movements have sought to limit women in certain social realms, they have symbolically coded those acts as fundamentally un-Christian and un-Western. To invoke the example in the introduction, the scholar Salida Jalalzai notes that comparing the Texas law about abortion with the Taliban's treatment of women demonstrates how "Islam and Muslims continue to be used in America as short-hand for misogyny, barbarism, and oppression"

(Jalalzai 2021). At the same time, she notes, such a position overlooks the very white, very Christian roots that are the basis of this Texas law.

Complicating the Stereotype Today

All of these issues lead us to consider the problematic assumption that liberal groups cannot generally be oppressive because their liberalism exempts them from oppressive behavior. To reiterate, this assumption misunderstands the relationship between religion and culture because we can't necessarily assume that groups called "liberal" don't create oppressive or unbalanced power systems even if it is often the case that more conservative ones have a tendency to do so. Remember the earlier discussion of Bourdieu and habitus: whatever is common in a culture will often be common in its dominant religious forms. What this effectively means is that when certain types of oppression are widely accepted by a culture (to the degree that they are often naturalized), they are likely to appear in all forms of religion, not just within conservative groups. To clarify, this is not to say that religious groups can never push against their culture's norms (or be *counter*cultural). It simply means that they usually don't, since the same people who comprise a culture are the very ones who are members of religious groups.

To complicate this stereotype, let's examine two different scenarios of religious groups that may defy these conventional categories in some way. The first example involves the deployment of gender norms in certain LGBTQ Christian churches. It is true that many Christian groups today have a very difficult relationship with the LGBTQ community, and for many such groups, that is a self-inflicted wound. In the American context, a large number of more conservative Christian movements (including many Catholics, alongside evangelicals and other conservative Protestants) have continued to reject the legitimacy of queer identities and relationships. Many more liberal Christian churches, on the other hand, have taken a much more affirming stance and have attempted to create cultures fully accepting of members of the LGBTQ community. Since the late 1960s, there have even been some denominations specifically catering to and/or comprising LGBTQ members (such as the Metropolitan Community Churches), which, if this were a matter of labels alone, could certainly be called liberal.

However, such simple labeling overlooks the role of culture in promoting norms even among groups that have historically been oppressed by them. Scholar J. Edward Sumerau's fieldwork demonstrates that even in a church that specifically catered to the LGBTQ population (and thus could be considered "liberal"), several of the gay men in the church who emerged as leaders appealed to a more conservative ideal of proper Christian manhood to justify their own leadership. They did this by demoting the lesbian members in the church as a bloc alongside certain gay men (namely, those that were effeminate and/or in nonmonogamous relationships). Sumerau effectively showed how this group of male leaders used complementarian assumptions about gender to create an organizational hierarchy. He called these efforts "compensatory manhood," or a desire to prove one's manhood and thus worth when the larger culture would not grant these men respect because they were gay (Sumerau 2012). Here, we have a group that on the surface might be called liberal but that still displays the oppressive power relationships often normalized within conservative groups, not to mention the larger culture.

A second example showcases how a group can engage in behaviors often labeled "liberal" even as its institutional agendas are often considered deeply conservative. The Hindutva movement is the name of a far-right movement in India that promotes an extreme form of Hindu nationalism. Although it has been affiliated with a series of political groups, it has been most recently embraced by factions within the dominant Bharatiya Janata Party (BJP). Hindutva is noteworthy for its position that Hindu cultural traditionalism should pervade Indian culture, and its general sense that religious diversity, on the whole, keeps Indians from realizing this traditionalist vision. These views help explain its promotion of policies that tend to deny non-Hindus (and particularly, Muslims) full civil rights, that equate Hindu identity with proper Indian citizenship, and that also tend to regard the ideal Indian woman as a wife and mother, not as an economically independent or powerful person. For a country and culture that has long struggled with a track record of rape, sexual assault, and domestic violence issues, these gendered images evoke the stereotype of conservative religion and oppression.

Ironically, however, it is these very images that Hindutva leaders have used to draw in many Indian women to their movement. Hindutva valorizes women who eschew feminism and who follow traditional gender norms by calling them "true women" whose decisions to identify primarily as wives and mothers unlock for them a moral status that other Indian women cannot match, not to mention positions them as the standard bearers and leaders for generations to come. Moreover, Hindutva leaders play up the concept of a Muslim threat by providing self-defense classes to women and engaging in rhetoric that depicts Muslim men as potential rapists. "Real" Indian (read = Hindu) women are thus promised increased social status if they prepare themselves both physically and intellectually to counter the threat to Mother India posed by these Muslim men. Far from a one-off or an outlier, we can find instances across the globe where women engage in publicly powerful roles within otherwise very conservative religious groups that may grant them limited authority (and considerable status) in some realms. At the same time, as in this case, the larger organization is often working toward platforms that more systematically constrain the power of women and sexual or gender minorities.

While, on the one hand, these examples show that nuances matter, we could also say, on the other hand, that they still display the larger trends Bourdieu discussed. Namely, what these examples show is that even when the group itself may exude a more "liberal" set of gendered practices, the larger conservative gender dynamics within that culture (in these cases, the promotion of stereotypically "masculine" gay men to positions of power, or giving women a voice so that they can contribute to their own structural disempowerment) ultimately win out. Both of these examples demonstrate that whatever has been normalized within a culture will tend to carry over into its religious groups, no matter what labels we might use to identify such groups ("conservative" or "liberal"). The question that follows, then, is whether the members of the group are aware of this dynamic and the degree to which they will use religious language to either justify or reject it.

Conclusion

We have seen that the stereotype that conservative religions oppress women (while liberal ones don't) is not as simple as it may appear on the surface. This is because the statement itself is filled with oversimplifications and assumptions that may not always accurately reflect how the social world operates.

So why does this stereotype persist? Like most stereotypes, this one is useful. From a more factual perspective, conservative religious groups tend to highlight gender and sexuality restrictions as a sign of what they claim is their piety, and, in this sense, the stereotype has some (limited) truth. To put it differently, the stereotype appears to be at least somewhat descriptive of how certain social groups behave.

But another use should not escape our notice. As mentioned previously, this stereotype has also been popular because it has been used to justify everything from colonial invasions to the present political distinctions between "good" and "bad" religion. This is where the accuracy of the stereotype becomes murkier. While stereotypes are almost always oversimplifications, this one is particularly prone to distortion because it is far more difficult to detect certain types of oppression that pervade cultures simply because they seem so normal. Much of this stereotype's power, then, lies in the gap between the obvious and the subtle.

9

"Religious Pluralism Gives Everyone a Voice"

Martha Smith Roberts

❝We are a nation of Christians and Muslims," President Barack Obama said in his first inaugural address in 2009, "Jews and Hindus, and non-believers." Like presidents before him, Obama's statement recognized the diversity of the American religious landscape and sought to amplify the voices of minority faiths. The president's rhetoric of recognition and inclusion is an example of religious pluralism. Religious pluralism is a response to religious diversity that claims to be tolerant and inclusive of the full participation of minority groups in a society. The idea that religious pluralism gives everyone a voice is an ideal that has deep roots in American culture and identity. Often, we see religious diversity acknowledged in public statements and performances of pluralism. Examples of this notion cross the political divide and span the last century and beyond. Obama, like all presidents since Clinton, has presided over Ramadan iftar dinners. He also held the first White House Passover Seder in 2009, and he was the first president to light the ceremonial oil lamp at a Diwali celebration (Manseau 2016). More recently, President Joseph Biden declared January 16, 2022, "Religious Freedom Day," stating,

> In my life, faith has always been a beacon of hope and a calling to purpose, as it is for so many Americans, and I believe that protecting religious freedom is as important now as it has ever been. We must continue our work to ensure that people of all faiths—or none—are treated as *full participants in society*, equal in rights and dignity. We can only fully realize the freedom we wish for ourselves by helping to ensure liberty for all. (2022, emphasis added)

The understanding of religious pluralism as the solution to the problems of religious diversity is the cliché that this chapter intends to deconstruct. It is not only politicians that use this rhetoric; the notion that religious pluralism gives everyone a voice and thus facilitates equality and full participation is a powerful cliché that dominates the discourse of American religious freedom. This cliché disguises the ways in which pluralism does not, and never has, given everyone a seat at the proverbial table. To the contrary, religious pluralism is an exercise in exclusion and the maintenance of dominant power structures.

Religious pluralism is conceived of in terms of a society's ability to tolerate, include, and allow the participation of all religious groups. When we discuss religious pluralism, it is often to refer to this ideal reality—the peaceful coexistence of diverse religious groups in a society where every group has a seat at the table and everyone's voices count. This ideal, while in many ways quite admirable, overlooks the negotiations of power and privilege inherent in pluralism. In the United States, religious pluralism is a part of the construction of national identity around religious freedom and equality. The motto *e pluribus unum*, "out of many one," is emblematic of this American ideal of unity in diversity. However, that notion belies the dominance and power of Protestant Christianity in American culture. Despite claims to include the voices of all religions, minority traditions have historically been silenced, sidelined, and excluded from American life and legal protections. The struggle by minority religious groups to have their voices heard and their beliefs and practices protected reveals the cracks in the pluralist rhetoric of progress and unity. The cliché that "religious pluralism gives everyone a voice" is meant to both generally sanction the ideal of pluralism as the solution to religious diversity and to specifically reinforce broader cultural values of equality, equity, and freedom of speech and religion. While religious pluralism is not the same thing as religious diversity, it is also not separable from the particular historical, social, and cultural contexts out of which both develop.

Religious pluralism is not only an issue in the United States. Religious diversity is a widespread phenomenon and it creates particular challenges for pluralism that are dependent on context. Outside of the United States, secular European nation-states also grapple with this concept, espousing pluralist and democratic ideals that claim to unite diverse groups into one broader culture, while often simultaneously imposing liberal Protestant notions of pluralism that exclude many from free practice of their traditions. Tomoko Masuzawa's now classic work *The Invention of World Religions: Or, How European Universalism Was Preserved in the Language of Pluralism* (2005) famously argues that pluralism is not a neutral ideal at all. Instead, it is the culmination of centuries of colonial endeavors that created and maintain a European cultural ideal as a normative, universal, and unbiased, way of life. While this chapter will focus on the context of the United States, American pluralism shares many characteristics with broader European pluralism, as well as with the variety of forms that pluralism takes outside of these spaces. Pluralism in India or Indonesia, for example, looks very different from the American or European versions but still relies on power dynamics of dominant and minority groups, conceptions of religion and secularity, and legal and political systems that define and manage acceptable forms of religiosity. The important thing to keep in mind is that context matters, and it has shaped cultural ideals around religious diversity in different ways in different spaces. This chapter will examine a few key places where the cliché "religious pluralism gives everyone a voice" appears in American popular culture and media and in scholarly literature. This chapter will ask you to consider the idea that religious pluralism is not a path to equity or inclusion but, rather, is a way of maintaining dominant power structures and policing difference.

Can Religious Pluralism Give Everyone a Voice?

To say that religious pluralism gives everyone a voice is to ignore the reality that it cannot possibly achieve that goal. If we take seriously the claim that pluralism itself emerged out of a European Christian context as an attempt to center that religious identity, we should immediately see the first problem inherent in the cliché. There is no way to give everyone a voice and center one voice simultaneously. And yet, this is the claim at the heart of pluralism: it can include all religious ideas, all religious identities, and all religious beliefs and practices in one shared social world. Even with a limited understanding of religious traditions throughout history, we know that many religions do not agree on fundamental understandings of the world and that they very rarely agree to disagree. Some religious traditions do not want pluralism. Others have contradictions with pluralism at the heart of their teachings, for example, they might silence particular voices within their own tradition (e.g., those of women, LGBTQIA2S+, and other religious groups). This essentially makes it impossible for pluralism to then claim that everyone has a voice; the inclusion of these groups does not erase their internal discrimination. If we try to salvage this idea of pluralism by claiming that it indeed only gives a voice to inclusive, open traditions, then again, it is not giving everyone a voice. In fact, this is the failure at the center of pluralist discourse and practice; there is no way to include all religious voices when some of those voices directly challenge pluralism itself. When we see claims that "pluralism gives everyone a voice," it is a good idea to ask a few important questions. Does "everyone" truly have a voice here? Who is actually included in this group?

Who is excluded from the conversation and why? And finally, who is doing the including and excluding in the first place? To say that "pluralism" can give a voice to others is a misrepresentation. It is more accurate to say that in the name of pluralism, the majority group grants power to minority groups that do not threaten the existence or goals of the majority. To begin the chapter by recognizing the fundamental impossibility of this cliché allows us to look at examples of religious pluralism at work in the world (in practice and theory) to see how and why they always, necessarily, fail to give everyone a voice.

Giving "Everyone a Voice" at the World's Parliament

The notion that everyone "has a voice" in a religiously pluralist culture can be seen in a variety of representations in advertising, media, and news. Often, diverse religious figures are used as markers of pluralism, as we saw in the list of religions mentioned by Obama previously. These lists and images of diverse groups constituting a pluralist ideal draw upon a quintessential moment in the development of modern pluralism in the United States: The World's Parliament of Religions in Chicago in 1893. This event, a part of the larger Columbian Exposition and World's Fair, was a symbol of pluralism at the end of the nineteenth century. The Parliament is an example of the beginnings of the cliché's claims that pluralism gives everyone a voice. It also offers us an example of how the act of giving diverse and minority traditions a voice is often a superficial attempt to subsume these traditions under the dominant religious voice of the majority.

Often referred to as "the dawn of religious pluralism," the World's Parliament of Religions showcased the religions and cultures of the world on an American stage, and it is often credited with introducing Eastern religions into American popular culture. Richard Hughes Seager's work on the Parliament and Exposition sheds light on the ways that public exhibition and celebration become platforms for American storytelling (1995). He notes that "diversity in unity" was the dominant ideal of the event's planners, who sought to highlight inclusivity, cooperation, and social progress. Speakers like Soyen Shaku, credited with bringing Zen Buddhism into American culture, and Swami Vivekananda, who introduced Hinduism and the Vedanta movement to Americans, left the Parliament celebrities and were instrumental in the spread of Eastern religions in the United States in the twentieth century. Shaku and Vivekananda became representative figures meant to show the diversity of religions at the Parliament and tout the success of pluralism. This version of the story emphasizes inclusion, but it should not let us miss the history of exclusion. The narrative of Eastern success occludes the lack of African American, African, and Latin American voices in the Parliament, as well as the discrimination against Chinese and Japanese participants. Under closer inspection, we see that the Parliament's organizers were unable to give everyone a voice, but more importantly we can see that the gesture of inclusion of minority groups was not meant to share power or promote religious equality. The Parliament in this sense is truly the "dawn of pluralism" in the United States, as it exemplifies the machinations of participatory pluralism: putting religious diversity on display while maintaining dominant structures of power.

The program designed by the Parliament's producers painted an image of both Protestant triumph and successful religious inclusion. Representatives from a variety of religious traditions and from around the world were invited to address the Parliament on behalf of their respective traditions. The event was truly an example of our cliché: "religious pluralism gives everyone a voice." And yet, already we can see that it was not exactly true that everyone had a voice. The greater good of pluralism was achieved through a labor of elision— an exclusion that rendered invisible the very violence that accomplished it. In addition, no matter how popular some of the Hindu and Buddhist speakers were, biases against Eastern religions would remain firmly enmeshed in American culture. Asian Exclusion laws and strict immigration quotas would keep most practicing Hindus and Buddhists from entering the country until after 1965. And many of those who were already in the United States in the late nineteenth and early twentieth centuries were not allowed to become naturalized citizens because the law extended this privilege only to "civilized white men." Thus it appears that even those groups who did "have a voice" in this pluralist program did not have any power or sway in the actual politics of religious freedom in the United States. In other words, this early example leads us to question the efficacy of this cliché and whether religious pluralism truly gives everyone a voice or simply uses their voices as placeholders in a superficial display of diversity.

Richard Seager's work outlines the ways in which the Parliament's pluralist goals were also taxonomic and hegemonic in nature. The Parliament became a display of the "unity in diversity" narrative. The ocular dimension of diversity—the spectacle of visuality—was very much a part of the Parliament's proceedings, and it remains a way that pluralism is conceptualized in American culture today. The very presence of diverse religious figures was used as evidence of progress toward a new "cosmopolitan" reality, one where the United States was represented as a uniquely progressive space of religious freedoms. In the newspaper reports from 1893, we see a fascination with this visual display of diversity as proof of the efficacy of religious pluralism:

It is the most cosmopolitan gathering in the history of man. If there is anything which draws a dividing line, it is religious beliefs and forms of worship, and to harmonize the religious faiths of the nations of the world would have been scorned down a half century ago. But such has been the advance in religious thinking that today representatives from China and Japan with their gaudily colored gowns, painted and bedecked prophets from India, Buddhist priests, Jews, Catholics and Protestants are all mingled together for one common purpose. "The Most Remarkable Gathering," *Democrat Northwest,* Napoleon, OH. (September 21, 1893)

However, if we examine this narrative of religious pluralism a bit more closely we will see that the producers of this event were not simply interested in religious freedom, but rather they hoped to show that the United States was a beacon of religious freedom because of its Protestant superiority. The producers of the fair had high hopes for the Parliament. In John Henry Barrows' 1892 progress report he claimed that "it is our expectation that the Parliament of Religions will be the most important, commanding, and influential, as surely it will be the most phenomenal fact of the Columbian Exposition" (Seager 1993, 5). The Parliament was seen by many as the "crown jewel" of the exposition, as it was meant to display the triumphs of American Protestantism as the highest point in the evolution of religion around the world.

The Congresses of the fair attempted to bridge evolutionary ideas and religious advancement as markers of human progress. Religious difference was reified as the religions of world were presented as discreet entities on a developmental path toward a similar goal. As Reverend James Bixby proclaimed in his address to the Congress on Evolution, "Evolution from lower to the higher, from the carnal to the spiritual, is not merely the path of man's past pilgrimage but the destiny to which the future calls him, for it is the path that brings his spirit into closest resemblance and most intimate union with the divine essence itself" (Rydell 68). At the Parliament, this evolutionary notion was, for many participants, a narrative of Christian triumph.

John Joseph Keane, rector of the Roman Catholic University in Washington, DC, delivered an address summing up the results of the Parliament as having "shown conclusively that the only worthy idea of God is that of monotheism" (Johnson 335). Reverend George Dana Boardman's address on the final day similarly argued, "Christ is the only unifier of mankind. Other religions are topographical; Christ is universal" (Johnson 335). In his closing address to the Parliament, Charles Carroll Bonney, president of the World's Congress Auxiliary, was equally celebratory of the fact that unity had been achieved at the conference, a unity very much defined by Christianity: "Henceforth the religions of the world will make war—not on each other, but on the giant evils that afflict mankind. Henceforth let all throughout the world who worship God and love their fellowmen join in the anthem of the angels: 'Glory to God in the Highest! Peace on earth, good will to men!'" (Johnson 337).

In contrast, Vivekananda's closing address was more cognizant of the Parliament's Christian-centered rhetoric as something other than positive. His moral lesson directly contradicted an evolutionary hierarchy of religions:

> If the Parliament of Religions has shown anything to the world it is this: It has proved to the world that holiness, purity, and charity are not the exclusive possessions of any church in the world, and that every system has produced men and women of the most exalted character. In the face of this evidence if anybody dreams of the exclusive survival of his own and the destruction of the others, I pity him from the bottom of my heart. (Barrows 1893: 170–1)

Vivekananda's not-so-subtle jab at the exclusivity of Christianity couched in the religious inclusion espoused by producers was not popular. In his commentary on the speech, Barrows noted, "Swami Vivekananda was always heard with interest by the Parliament, but very little approval was shown to some of the sentiment expressed in his closing address" (1893: 171). As a Hindu attendee, Vivekananda was perhaps more acutely aware of the failure of the Parliament to fully embody utopian goals of tolerance and inclusion. However, that failure of tolerance was not as widely recognized at the time, as many of the closing remarks of the Parliament evidence. While inviting representatives from various traditions to speak did mark a progressive gesture of inclusion in the late nineteenth century, giving everyone a voice was not meant to give everyone a voice, nor everyone's voice equal weight. It would seem, then, that unity in diversity was not a motto of full participation and equality. Instead, the Parliament (and the Midway of World's Fair itself) was a site for the public construction of a particular narrative about religion and human development that promised participation and equality, but could ultimately only deliver it to only a select few. Producers and visitors were participating in the construction of normative frameworks that excluded and degraded non-white and non-Christian humans in the name of unity, knowledge, and progress.

The Parliament is still referred to as the dawn of religious pluralism in the United States, and it remains an important milestone in the narrative of progress toward greater inclusion of minority religions. The cliché that religious pluralism gives everyone a voice persists, and, in fact, counts the Parliament as a successful moment in the history of pluralism. This kind of multicultural production of diversity is one that is inextricably tied to the present-day notion of religious pluralism in the United States. Contemporary moments repeat this imagery. Not only the formal continued gatherings of the Parliament of the

World's Religions but also informal interfaith movements, religious advisory boards, and even world religions courses display religious diversity to prove the existence of equity and equality in the larger American landscape. For example, at the most recent Parliament, held virtually in 2021, there were a variety of diverse figures and voices featured. The Dalai Lama may be the most well-known, but there are many speakers from around the world representing diverse religious traditions and holding titles like bishop, holiness, reverend, swami, rabbi, dharma master, eminence, and more. Much like the White House hosting diverse religious ceremonies and recognizing minority religious holidays, these *displays of diversity* function to draw attention to the inclusion of previously excluded traditions. In each of these iterations, we can see the idea of "religious pluralism giving everyone a voice" on display. Diversity on display is a key component in the creation of this cliché, but there are many historical threads that have contributed to this idea, including the scholarship on pluralism itself.

Scholarship on American Pluralism

The language around giving all groups "a seat at the table" or "a voice in the conversation" is used to support the ideal of pluralism as inclusive and equitable. This kind of language assumes that creating space for minority religions to not only exist but also participate is the key to equality. Religious pluralism as well as the narrative of religious freedom has been an important way of telling the American story for centuries. Early accounts of American culture by historians and in textbooks highlight the exceptional nature of religious tolerance in the United States. In fact, the "founding myth" of the United States is centered on the story of Pilgrims looking for freedom from religious persecution and finding it on the shores of the New World. All of these narratives have contributed to a notion of pluralism as a quintessential form of religious freedom for all. It is the *story* of religious freedom (not the reality of those claims) that informs our cliché.

This American "founding myth" is a story that highlights the colonies and early republic as a space where settlers sought and found refuge from the religious persecution of violence of Europe. The story continues into the founding of the nation, the Declaration of Independence, Constitution, and the First Amendment religious protections that "Congress shall make no law respecting an establishment of religion or prohibiting the free exercise thereof." From there, the story expands to include more and more diversity, and it boasts of the presence of temples, synagogues, mosques, gurdwaras, and more. These spaces of worship become additional symbols of the ways in which the American landscape has made room for everyone. How can the United States not be a pluralist nation when it is so obviously diverse? John Corrigan and Lynn Neal write that it is this story of the triumph of religious freedom and pluralism, this "founding myth," that has proliferated in textbooks that recount the story of American religious history for generations of Americans. They trace this narrative from colonial commentators through nineteenth-century texts and well into contemporary America. They argue that this story has had an enormous impact on Americans' understanding of religious pluralism, as religious intolerance gradually disappeared from textbooks.

> In the late nineteenth and early twentieth centuries, the textbook narrative stressed toleration and harmony as a longstanding historical fact and juxtaposed it with early colonial instances of intolerance in order to drive home the point of the wholesale realization of the idea of freedom written into the Constitution. . . . Such narratives fashioned American's thinking about their history, and above all about the absence of religious intolerance since the founding of the United States. Religious intolerance has been all but written out of the story for a century or more. (2020: 7–8)

Scholarship and popular sentiment are bound together in this cliché. It is often the case that Americans do not simply learn about religious diversity, they learn about diversity as pluralism. Discussions of religious pluralism in the United States have been a feature of scholarship throughout American history. However, starting in the twentieth century, participatory pluralism became the dominant characterization of the ideals of religious life and diversity. The growth of religious diversity since the early 1970s has also contributed to the breadth of research on immigrant and minority religions and new religious movements. Three authors whose work best represents this kind of interpretive view of pluralism and its development in America include Diana Eck, an ecumenical theologian, and the historians Charles Lippy and William Hutchison.

A scholar of Hinduism with an interest in ecumenical-theological projects, Diana Eck fashioned a narrative of American pluralist history that moved the United States from a "Christian country" to "the world's most religiously diverse nation" (Porterfield 2013: 33). Both her work with Harvard's Pluralism Project and her book A New Religious America highlight the existence of diversity from early America to the present, challenging narratives that would call the United States a Christian nation and taking issue with interpretations of diversity that called for the loss of cultural identity through assimilation models. Eck's work with the Pluralism Project focused on documenting diversity's existence, but she was also theorizing its significance and looking for its meaning in American culture. This interpretive framework posited that religious diversity was a central feature in the creation and maintenance of a national identity; it was a principle grounded in the very founding of the United States.

Eck cites three ways in which Americans have approached their ever-broader cultural and religious diversity: exclusion, assimilation, and pluralism. For Eck, exclusionists see the unity of American culture as threatened by outsiders and immigrants and have determined that exclusion of these groups is the way to manage difference (including exclusion from civic participation and from the culture in general, often in the form of restrictive immigration laws). Assimilation (or inclusiveness) does not prohibit all participation, but it does require minority groups to shed their differences and become assimilated into the normative culture. Finally, Eck's understanding of *pluralism* sees it as a culture in which unity is shaped by the encounter of many diverse groups with their differences intact; and the only requirement a pledge to the common civic demands of citizenship (2001: 47). She sums up these three responses to diversity as: "Stay home, or go home" in exclusion, "come, but leave your differences behind" in assimilation, and "come and be yourselves" in pluralism. For Eck, the history of American religious diversity can be interpreted through a lens of increasing progress toward this final form of pluralism (Eck 2001: 47). Eck's understanding of pluralism is very much in line with our cliché; pluralism is a positive force that brings America closer and closer to its equitable founding ideals.

The proposal that it is not only the demographics of diversity but also the meaning of diversity (in other words, pluralism) that has shifted in the United States has been forwarded by historians as well. What these theories all share is a teleological narrative of progress. In other words, they see religious pluralism as a positive force that both sets America apart and moves it toward its destiny. Charles H. Lippy offers another account of pluralism in American history, with special attention to the twentieth century. In *Pluralism Comes of Age: American Religious Culture in the Twentieth Century* (2000), Lippy offers insight into pluralism's development in the United States, while simultaneously exemplifying some of the difficulties inherent in the pluralist project. Lippy traces three major historical moments in the trajectory of pluralism. Unlike Eck, however, his descriptions of these phases are not based on the type of pluralist strategy that dominated. Instead, he describes these phases in terms of the dominant, mainstream religious groups of the time: Protestant denominational pluralism, Protestant-Catholic-Jewish pluralism, and a radical pluralism that emerged post-1965 (2000, 16–17).

The first two phases of pluralism, for Lippy, have a strong hegemonic order (either the Protestant mainstream or the Protestant-Catholic-Jewish mainstream), which other groups had to engage with and in some way conform to in order to enter American culture. *Radical pluralism*, in Lippy's history, is a space where minorities can enter and engage on their own terms, free of a hegemonic majority (122–123). He traces increased acceptance of religious diversity within existing traditions, personal expression and religious choice, and new traditions, and he includes all of this in the framework of pluralism. For Lippy, that framework is a larger trajectory that began in the early republic with a pluralism of multiple Protestant groups and "comes of age" in the early twenty-first century with a new coexistence of a vast variety of beliefs, practices, faiths, and worldviews that populate the American landscape. Like Eck, Lippy too sees contemporary pluralism as a space where "everyone has a voice."

William R. Hutchison's work *Religious Pluralism in America: The Contentious History of a Founding Ideal* (2003) is a good example of the ways in which early twenty-first-century scholarship has attempted to make sense of the nuances of both *popular notions* of American religious exceptionalism and the *scholarship* that has created and perpetuated them. Hutchison deliberately separates the fact of diversity from the ideal of pluralism. Acknowledging the existence of *religious diversity* from early America onward, Hutchison lays out the development of *religious pluralism* (the way diversity is understood and dealt with) in three main phases in American history: *toleration, inclusion, and participation*. He posits that these are the central frameworks through which Americans have attempted to reconcile differences and achieve pluralism.

Hutchison's work is a Protestant-centered narrative, which reminds us that the concept of pluralism is a construction of a particular majority that is coming to terms with the "others" that coexist in American society. Hutchison highlights the negotiated nature of the ideal of pluralism and the fact that it is a construction of "meaningful diversity" that is not static but changes over time in relation to historical and social contexts. Understanding pluralism is actually understanding the ways in which the dominant white, Protestant, American culture assigns meaning to diversity. Hutchison's model is useful for understanding our cliché as a part of a larger pattern of meaning-making that contributes to the social construction of religious "others" in public culture. His descriptions of *participatory pluralism* reinforce the idea that our cliché is the dominant ideal through which contemporary Americans understand pluralism. And that that ideal is inseparable from the dominant Protestant ethos in American culture.

Eck, Lippy, and Hutchison all utilize three-phase models to describe a larger movement in pluralism over the course of American history as an expansion in religious diversity, but more importantly, an expansion in the boundaries of acceptance of diversity. In each of these accounts, pluralism becomes a more active, inclusive ideal; in other words, these are all teleologies, all narratives of progress. Eck, Lippy, and Hutchison make clear the fact that pluralism is not static over time, but that it has indeed changed in response to shifts in diversity and hegemony. However, ultimately, all of these authors see a trajectory of pluralism that culminates in the radical, participatory pluralism of the twenty-first century, and all see pluralism as a continuous, constantly expanding presence in American life. Because of that, these scholars also contribute to the cliché that religious pluralism gives everyone a voice. They remain tethered to the notion that pluralism will eventually "work" even though it has consistently failed in the past.

While *historians* have chronicled the changes in the American religious landscape over time, *sociologists* have attempted to make sense of those changes in relation to larger sociological frameworks. Current sociological theory often deals with the issue of religious diversity in terms of secularization and rational choice theory. The possible significance of pluralism is thus seen in terms of either a secularized, modernized loss of religious power in civil society (secularization) or a market-driven increase in religious choices in the modern world (rational choice theory). Early theory, however, focused on American religious diversity in terms of immigration and assimilation models. Will Herberg's 1955 *Protestant, Catholic, Jew: An Essay in American Religious Sociology* is one of the most well-known sociological works to attempt to document the phenomenon of pluralism, though many before him had studied assimilation and generational shifts in immigrant communities in relation to religious affiliation (Robert Park, Marcus Hansen, Ruby Jo Reeves Kennedy, Horace Kallen, and Randolph Bourne). Herberg's "triple melting pot" can be seen as an early version of our cliché in many ways, though a limited version of it. In his work, only Protestants, Catholics, and Jews had the potential to have a voice in the American religious landscape, and only through assimilation to the "American way of life." Notably, he did not think that any other religious groups could be fully "American," listing Buddhists, Muslims, and even atheists, as unable to make the cut. Post-1965 immigration trends would soon render his theory incomplete, but the idea that multiple groups could be considered "American religions" is one that persists in the cliché today.

Unlike early twentieth-century sociological studies on immigrant assimilation to cultural norms, contemporary scholarship considers the meanings that will be assigned to diversity within the larger logic of a participatory pluralism in the American context. In his 2003 essay "The Problem of Pluralism," David Machacek describes the move from "assimilation to appreciation" that sums up this theoretical trajectory. Like William Hutchison, Machacek proposes that new religious pluralism is more than diversity; it is meaningful diversity. New religious pluralism and the scholarship surrounding the post-1965 shifts in the American religious landscape claim to recognize and value diversity over assimilation. The religious pluralism in our cliché claims that it is not a "melting pot" model that seeks to give everyone the same voice. Like Diana Eck's "come and be yourselves" ideal, this pluralist cliché is represented as the most accepting of difference, the most willing to keep diversity intact, and thus the most progressive form of religious liberty. These scholarly claims are in fact also doing the work of our cliché. They propose an inclusive appreciation and meaningful cultural exchange; however, they are also always involved in the work of power. Who is appreciated? Which exchanges are meaningful and thus appropriate to include? Inclusivity is always a negotiation of power. To say that minority religions in the United States can "come as they are" and fully participate in American democracy is simply untrue. The work of our cliché, and of these scholars, is to make this process of exclusion seem natural and even equitable. Pluralism is inextricably tied to the power of the dominant religious group in a society. Even if it is seeking to include, it is never seeking to overthrow the balance of power. Pluralism only works if there is a "dominant" group to engage with "minority" groups. In the United States, pluralism relies on the maintenance of the Protestant cultural framework. It is not trying to give everyone an equal seat at the table. It is interested in keeping majority groups at the head of the table.

Lest we start to believe pluralism's contradictions are somehow exclusive to American history and scholarship, it is important to note that the study of religion more broadly has also had to reckon with the problem of pluralism. Here, we can cite the work of one of the earliest scholars in the field of religious studies, Rudolf Otto. Otto was a nineteenth-century German theologian whose famous book *The Idea of the Holy* argued that at the core of all religious experience lay something that humans describe as holy or sacred, and what he would call "the *numinous.*" Humans who experience the *numinous* have a feeling he termed *mysterium tremendum et fascinans,* a simultaneous attraction and repulsion to this external power. This human experience, or feeling, of the power of the holy, becomes the center of his investigation of religion, and he proceeds to attempt to trace this phenomenon through human history. However, Otto's work offers an example of the failures of pluralism in the study of religion. The Holy represents the ineffable and irreducible element of religion for Otto; it is a clear overplus of meaning, one that is simultaneously a priori (prior to experience) and sui generis (entirely irreducible, a distinct category of meaning); the holy is also the sine qua non, the essential substance of religious experience. Even after arguing for this understanding of the holy as prior to human experience, irreducible to other phenomena, and inextricable from *any* religious experience, he goes on to posit an evolutionary theory of religion that places Christianity at the top of the hierarchy as the "most developed" form of religion or experience of the numinous.

Craig Martin's *A Critical Introduction to the Study of Religion* reminds us of the structures of power at work in Otto's theory. While Otto's definition of religion "as a sensing or feeling of 'the Holy'" may seem quite benign,

Martin notes that "his definition was designed to present Christianity—and, more specifically, Protestant Christianity—as the most 'rational' religion and 'unsurpassable'" (9). Although the experience of religion is nonrational, for Otto, "Christians sensed or felt 'the Holy' and put that feeling into rational terms better than any other religion" (9). Religion also became "a tool for ranking cultures and putting his favorite at the top," and Otto was thus "reinventing the definition of words to serve his interests, thereby presenting his culture as superior to all other cultures" (9). Martin's work is a reminder that no scholar or theory exists outside of the social and cultural power relations of their time. With that in mind, it helps to contextualize Otto historically.

Critiques of Pluralist Paradigms in Scholarship and Culture

In her 2005 *The Invention of World Religions: Or, How European Universalism Was Preserved in the Language of Pluralism*, Tomoko Masuzawa examines the ways in which the rhetoric of pluralism is a way to preserve power, not necessarily to share participation equally. Though she is not focusing on the American context particularly, Masuzawa raises important questions about the use of pluralism to conceal other agendas. Along those lines, scholars like Russell McCutcheon (*The Domestication of Dissent* [2005]) and Tim Murphy ("Religious Defamation and Radical Pluralism as Challenges to the Scholar of Religion" [2005]) challenge the notion of pluralism itself, noting that the very inclusion of some groups is always defining particular parameters for acceptable religion (thus forcing the groups to fit them) and excluding others whose religions do not meet these standards. As McCutcheon notes, "This rhetoric of the big picture, the unity that encompasses all diversity, the synthesis that unites all opposites, in which one attempts to attain full understanding by listening carefully to all of the voices, may be one of the most powerful political techniques we've yet come up with to silence just some voices while amplifying others" (2005, 27). Religious pluralism cannot possibly give everyone a voice. By claiming to do so, pluralism is centering particular voices as authentic religions and excluding and maligning others as themselves intolerant, radical, extreme, or simply not authentic religions (2005, 30).

Because the voices centered in pluralism are white Protestant voices, this applies to minority religious groups and religions of racial minorities as well. Many scholars have noted that while the theories of assimilation and choice generally work for white Americans, they fail in the case of racial minorities. As works like Ronald Takaki's *A Different Mirror* (1993), Joseph Cheah's *Race and Religion in American Buddhism* (2011), and Khyati Y. Joshi's *New Roots in America's Sacred Ground* (2006) illustrate, bodies that bear the mark of racial difference do not follow similar patterns of assimilation into American culture. Following the scholarship of Edward Said and Omi and Winant, works like those of Cheah and Joshi focus on the ways in which the identity of religious and racial others (particularly those in the context of the "new pluralism" of post-1965 America) have been constructed in relation to the dominant white Protestant American culture. These recent studies support the theory that while pluralism may espouse a neutral playing ground for all religions, racialized minority faiths are not allowed to fully participate in American religious freedom. These examples remind us that the displays of religious and racial diversity that are so often used to evidence the claims of pluralism inevitably do not produce the inclusivity they promise.

The failures of pluralism are perhaps most visible in the courts, where minority groups struggle to claim their "voice" in the American legal system. Lori G. Beaman's article "The Myth of Pluralism, Diversity, and Vigor: The Constitutional Privilege of Protestantism in the United States and Canada" (2003) challenges the sunny view of pluralism by arguing that sociologists have been too anxious to take diversity for granted and too quick to conflate the choices of the religious marketplace with a meaningful diversity. For Beaman, religious choice exists only within a narrow range of products. This is a range of products dominated by the Protestant mainstream, in which the diverse groups remain marginal. To prove this phenomenon, Beaman cites four representative court cases illustrative of the ways in which boundaries are maintained and the religious mainstream preserved when challenged by indigenous claims, immigrant religions, marginalized Christian groups, and new religious movements. In each case, the nondominant tradition involved challenged the status quo and lost. Beaman cites the well-known case of *Employment Division v. Smith* (494 U.S. 872), "in which the U.S. Supreme Court rejected free exercise claims of two drug rehabilitation organization employees who had ingested peyote for sacramental purposes. The two were subsequently denied unemployment compensation, essentially because they were dismissed 'with cause'" (319). In *Bhinder v. CN*, we have an example of immigrant religious discrimination upheld by the Canadian Courts. In this case, "a Canadian National Railway employee refused to wear a hard hat at his place of work because he was a Sikh who could wear only a turban. The Supreme Court of Canada upheld Bhinder's dismissal, stating that the requirement to wear a hard hat was a bona fide occupational requirement" (319). Similarly, in the two cases of marginalized Christian groups (a Quaker who paid a portion of her taxes to a Peace Tax Fund that aligned with her religious pacifism) and new religious movements (the raid, search, and seizure of documents at a Scientology head office that resulted in fraud charges), we see that the courts always ruled to limit the free exercise and religious freedom of minority groups.

In each of these cases, Beaman argues, the shared issue is "the request for protection of religious freedom as a 'special' circumstance requiring accommodation" when this very notion of accommodation "reinforces the notion that minority groups are different" (321). This is an important critique of the clichés surrounding religious pluralism. The notion of giving everyone a voice is of course only referring to minority traditions and those at the margins. Mainstream and dominant religious voices create the backdrop of religious normalcy that is rooted in Protestant hegemony; they do not need to be given a voice (321). Pluralism *relies on* the existence of discreet minority religious traditions that are marginalized in the social world; it does not seek to change this dynamic. And the courts consistently uphold this arrangement.

In their 2010 volume *After Pluralism: Reimagining Religious Engagement*, Courtney Bender and Pamela E. Klassen interrogate pluralism and what they say are the "imaginative failures" at its core (22). Here, they are referring to some of the same issues that Beaman cites above, including the inherent tensions between pluralism's simultaneous *reliance upon* and *need to eradicate* the power differentials between dominant and minority groups. Bender and Klassen note that "Pluralism, variously specified as cultural, political, legal, or religious, has come to represent a *powerful ideal* meant to resolve the question of how to get along in a conflict-ridden world" (2010, 1; emphasis added). I would go even further and argue that pluralism is a paradigmatic way in which Americans understand religious diversity. This pluralist paradigm dominates American conceptions of diversity in that it actively constructs, maintains, and limits the kind of relationships that Americans believe should exist between religious groups. Pluralism fails when the *ideal* is mistaken for the *real*, and inevitable, solution to resolving difference. Giving everyone a voice is not an achievable task. And although the *participatory* pluralism that seeks to bring all voices to the table is a marker of progress from earlier, particularly pre-twentieth-century goals of the assimilation and tolerance of minority groups that paid little to no attention to their full participation, it is not the only solution, nor is it the best or ideal solution.

What does it mean to critique the cliché that "religious pluralism gives everyone a voice"? Recognizing and critiquing the problems of this cliché does not mean destroying the ideal of pluralism, but understanding it as a mechanism of power. As Bender and Klassen note, pluralism is a "dominant frame" that guides our understanding of diversity in contemporary American culture (2). Studying the history of pluralism and the ways in which a pluralist paradigm is at work in our field and in the American cultural consciousness will result in a recognition of religious diversity that is both self-reflexive and open to new possibilities. While good in theory, if presented as a neutral, easy, or obvious strategy, this cliché can quickly slip into a dangerous space. As we seek to impart the lessons of diversity learned over the course of American history, we must remember the impossibility of the *ideal* encounter. The messiness of religious diversity overlaps with the differences of race, class, and gender. The on-the-ground experiences of diverse Americans do not fit into one magnificent narrative of progress. The conflicts and violence that define the struggles to create a place for diverse voices and policies continue to happen, as do the violent acts of overt discrimination that seek to stop it from happening. For these reasons and more, it is important to take seriously the critiques of the pluralist paradigm, even as we look for ways to realize a society where a more neutral space of encounter could happen (Roberts 2013). "Religious pluralism gives everyone a voice" is a cliché that sums up the hopefulness of the American ideal of religious freedom and equality. That hopefulness serves to distract from reality. Our cliché conceals the real-world negotiations of power that silence minority voices in the service of maintaining dominant cultural and religious hierarchies. Like most clichés, it is an overused and underexamined statement that has lost its connection to reality and its originality or ingenuity. It reflects and supports a pluralist paradigm which serves to limit, not expand, our understanding of religion, freedom, and inclusion.

10

"Cults Are Not Real Religions"

Matthew C. Baldwin

In popular usage, the word "cult" is almost a cliché unto itself. The term is used widely, with too much ease, and with its significance and appropriateness seemingly taken for granted, by all kinds of speakers and writers: members of the general public, journalists, politicians, and even academics.

In its everyday usage, "cult" ordinarily has strongly negative connotations and is often a term of disparagement. Except in instances when the term refers to culturally marginal arts that appeal strongly to limited but devoted audiences, a speaker or writer will most often direct the word "cult" against groups and/or individuals who are being derided as unthinking, marginal, strange, aberrant, dangerous, or otherwise "beyond the pale." Groups described as "cults" are often accused of being "psychologically, emotionally, and physically" "oppressive" or "damaging" to group members or society at large (e.g., in Allen 2017).

For a good example of this kind of usage, consider an August 2020 instance in which the Nagaland Baptist Church Council (located in Northern India) issued a letter warning of the spread of "a cult, called 'Church of Almighty God' from China" (see *Sentinel* 2020). The "Church of Almighty God" is a small but international movement, is currently banned in China, and has been labeled as a "cult" by a wide variety of Chinese, Indian, and British news outlets. It was founded by Zhao Weishan in 1990 and later in 2014 became virally notorious after Church members brutally murdered a woman who rebuffed their efforts as proselytization in a McDonalds restaurant (see BBC 2015 and *OpIndia* 2020).

Negative traits associated with the word "cult" include especially fanaticism and unreasoning or unwavering devotion to a group or leader. When a group is led by a charismatic figure, the term "cult" can imply that the leader's influence over followers is absolute and possibly the result of deliberate deception or even "mind control." People will speak of cult members being "under a spell" or "brainwashed," perhaps in need of some kind of "deprogramming."

Popular writers do not hesitate to apply the term both *literally*, in reference to minority religious groups, and *analogically*, in reference to other forms of allegedly extreme belief, practice, or allegiance. As an example of the literal sense, consider a list of 100 books about "cults and oppressive religious sects," published on the popular review site *Book Riot* by avid reader and online reviewer Elizabeth Allen. Her list includes books about Scientology, the Branch Davidians, Fundamentalist Latter-Day Saints, the Unification Church, the People's Temple, Christian Science, right-wing Christian fundamentalist organizations, and many others (Allen 2017). As an example of the analogical sense, throughout 2021 and 2022, the *Washington Post* printed numerous editorials by the political commentator Jennifer Rubin in which she refers to the supporters of former US president Donald Trump as "the MAGA cult." (For a critical discussion of this trope, see Mosurinjohn 2020.)

Journalistic outlets that have and seemingly continue to publish stories that label groups as "cults" include *The New York Times*, *Time*, *Foreign Policy Magazine*, *The Atlantic*, *The Guardian*, *Vanity Fair*, *Rolling Stone*, *Vox*, *The History Channel*, *Cosmopolitan*, and many others.

Popular usage of the word "cult" is usually but not always linked in some way to uses of the term "religion." Both "religion" and "cult" imply groupings of people who adhere to specific beliefs and practices. When any group has formal structures, practices, and ideas that are deemed comparable with similar patterns observed in other groups commonly described as "religious," it is likely someone will describe it as a "religion," or even, if it considered somehow insidious, a "cult." Sometimes, even a movement whose adherents would disavow the label "religion" for themselves will be labeled as a "cult." An example is the corporate leadership training program and criminal sex trafficking organization known as NXIVM ("Nexium"), which has been widely labeled as a cult—thanks in part to the reporting of *The New York Times*, and in part to the highly visible anti-NXIVM activism and filmmaking of the actress Catherine Oxenberg (Meyer 2017; Moynihan 2019; Robinson 2019; Peck 2020). Arguably, there is a deliberate purpose served when people choose to label a group as a "cult" instead of referring to it as a "religion" or as a "religious group." While "religion" remains a more neutral descriptor, the word "cult" has an almost exclusively negative tone. "Religions" may be good, but "cults" never are.

Ordinary usage of the term does convey the idea of a similarity between "cults" and "religions," and yet calling something a "cult" usually implies it is different than a mere "religion." In a way, then, the popular usage of the term "cult" already contains and implies the clichéd idea, which is the subject of this essay: "cults are not real religions." This cliché maintains that a cult may look like a religion, and that cults in general might resemble religions, but cults are not "really" religions. Clichés about religion always need to be corrected. But this cliché is doubly problematic. Let's unpack and debunk its problematic assumptions.

What's a Real Religion, Anyway?

First, the cliché is problematic because it assumes that people have the ability to distinguish between the "real" and "fake" forms of "religion." But researchers in anthropology, sociology, and religious studies cannot even agree exactly on how to define "religion," let alone distinguish its "true" and "false" forms. A wide variety of definitions of "religion" have been proposed by scholars working in religious studies, and many of these can be applied as easily to "cults" as they can be applied to "real religions." Thus, many so-called "cults" include "culturally patterned interaction with culturally postulated superhuman beings" (Spiro 1966, 96); or "a system of general compensators based on supernatural assumptions" (Stark and Bainbridge 1979, 121); or "discourse[s] . . . that speak of things eternal and transcendent with an authority equally transcendent and eternal" (Lincoln 1996, 225); or "belief in a transcendent reality . . . and the connected aspiration to a transformation which goes beyond ordinary human flourishing" (Taylor 2007, 510); or "social practices authorized by reference to a superempirical reality" (Schilbrack 2013, 313). On all such definitions, most so-called "cults" *are* "religions."

Hidden Normative Assumptions

This issue points to a second, larger, and even more troubling problem with the cliché. The idea that "cults are not real religions" contains a set of hidden normative assumptions concerning the role that "religion" should play in human life. To borrow a phrase from Craig Martin, this cliché *masks the hegemony* (or *cultural dominance)* of one particular conception of religion (Martin 2015). The commonsense notion that "cults" are "fake," "bad," or "false" forms of "religion" depends on a particular set of ideas about "religion" that just happen to fit in well with the social order that dominates in our modern, "liberal," and "secular" nation-state.

"Religion," on this account of it, consists of a system of private and elective beliefs associated with self-discipline, good citizenship, and pro-social behavior. This ecumenical understanding of "religion" just happens to be modeled on (but is by no means restricted to) the forms of Protestant Christianity that have historically prevailed in the United States. This form of "religion" fits in well with the individualist, liberal, capitalist culture of the modern West. As President Dwight D. Eisenhower once famously claimed (in 1952), "our form of government has no sense unless it is founded in a deeply felt religious faith, and I don't care what it is" (Henry 1981, 41). Unless it's a "cult" of course!

Eisenhower's disavowed interest in the particulars of religious faith, practice, or identity betrays the basic assumption that *religion per se* is a social good, a part of the bedrock of the Western cultural order. If this is true, then any form of life that *seems* religious but which threatens the social order, cannot, ipso facto, be called "religion."

While masquerading as a scientific category useful for classifying particular movements and sects, the word "cult" actually turns those using the term into unwitting insiders to a normative discourse about what is and is not socially acceptable in "religion." Popular usage of the term has a latent function: it delineates the boundaries of proper or normative social conduct. The term "cult" is a socially useful tool (for some actors) precisely because it enables people to distinguish between recognized groups, whose functioning is regarded as mainly pro-social and more or less culturally acceptable, and unrecognized groups, whose functioning is regarded as antisocial and unacceptable.

Studying popular discourses about "cults" can thus reveal a great deal about how social actors manufacture and maintain normative ideas through systems of classification. It shows one way that "secular" Western societies have actually insulated the concept of "religion" from critique. The idea that "cults are not real religions" effectively disavows the darker sides of "religion," projecting them onto "non-religion."

The History of the Word "Cult"

The term "cult" has not always had the connotations that it mostly has today. To understand more fully how the term functions as it does in contemporary usage, we have to survey the history of how the word has been used in the English language and the role it has played in society.

English writers began to use the term "cult" in the seventeenth century. It entered the English language via French, but its origins are in ancient Latin. The ancient Latin term *cultus* had a broad range of meanings related to farming, education, training, care, service, and maintenance. Ancient Romans also used *cultus* to refer to ritualized institutional practices associated with the worship of (or service to) the gods. It was from this last sense of the term that

French and English writers borrowed when they first coined the word "cult." Early English writers thus used the word "cult" to signify institutional systems of worship devoted to a god or gods.

Today, the word "cult" is still often used in this original sense, particularly among classicists (scholars who study ancient Greek and Roman writings), historians, and religious studies scholars who work on the ancient world and non-Christian traditions. It is easy to find examples of contemporary scholars of religion who continue to use the word "cult" in this way (a great many examples could easily be cited; here are three: Murray 2009; Robinson and Sironen 2013; and Latham 2020).

Over time, English writers began to extend their use of the word "cult" in the direction of today's more familiar and popular senses of the term. As early as the eighteenth century, satirical English writers began occasionally to use the term "cult" *analogically* to refer to excessive admiration of or obsessive devotion to something (the *Oxford English Dictionary* cites such a usage from a 1711 book by Lord Shaftebury). Such usage of the term became even more common in the nineteenth century. This type of analogical usage continues to this day, particularly with reference to elements of culture, including music, film, fashion, and, occasionally, politics. A simple internet search for phrases such as "cult classic" or "cult of personality" will reveal a widespread pattern of writers making analogical use of the term, drawing on its implications of devotion and fandom in politics and art.

As an aside, it must be stated that although this last-mentioned usage of the word "cult" can arguably be construed as "positive" (as when fans rave about a "cult film"), it is important to note that this "positive" meaning relies on connotative irony. The linguistic distinction performed by applying the label "cult" relies on this presumed structure of opposition between center and periphery. Labeling media as "cult" happens precisely because the term allows for differentiation from "the mainstream." That which is disdained by the public may be loved by a few loyal followers, but by definition, "cult classics" aren't to everybody's liking. Labeling such work "cult" embraces the marginality, eccentricity, obscurity, relative smallness of following, and often comparably transgressive content of such fare. Embracing the positive valence of the term is comparable to embracing the descriptor "punk" as a positive term by fans of "punk music." Consider the case of that classic of "cult classics," *The Rocky Horror Picture Show* (Sharman 1975), a film focused on that "sweet transvestite from Transsexual, Transylvania," Frank N. Furter, a character played with campy comic audacity by Tim Rice. Almost fifty years after its first release, this film is still shown with ritual regularity on weekend nights in late-night second-run theaters, drawing small crowds of devoted fans, who often dress up in costume, and among various other antics loudly chant lines from the film during the showing (Itkis 2015).

Toward the end of the nineteenth century, many writers began to use the term "cult" more frequently in the negatively charged way that characterizes most of its uses today. The *Oxford English Dictionary* (OED) defines this negative sense of the term "cult" as "[a] relatively small group of people having (esp. religious) beliefs or practices regarded by others as strange or sinister, or as exercising excessive control over members." The earliest cited usage of the term in this sense as found in the OED is from 1875. Interestingly, subsequent examples of this usage come mainly from American sources.

Lexicographic data allows us to argue that people began to use the word "cult" in the ordinary sense much more frequently only during the last century. A google n-gram graph showing the relative frequency of the word "cult" appearing in English-language books during the years 1800–2010 illustrates this point. An n-gram shows that usage of the term "cult" was flat until the last quarter of the nineteenth century. It then began to skyrocket, peaking in the early 1990s. In 1993, a published book was around thirty-five times as likely to use the word "cult" as was a book published in 1872. (The same graph shows that the usage of the word in books has since declined, though it remains relatively high compared to the mid-nineteenth century and before.)

What caused this increase in the relative frequency of usage of the word "cult" among twentieth-century English writers? Though the full history of the term's genealogy has yet to be written—and is beyond the scope of this essay—widespread use of the word "cult" emerged simultaneously with the huge cultural shifts that have characterized late modernity. It is only with reference to this world-historical context that ordinary uses of "cult" can be explained.

The Idea of the "Cult" in Western Modernity

Beginning in the seventeenth century, European societies exploited technological and economic advantages to establish a world-spanning system of colonization and trade in goods and slaves. This expansion of "colonialist" power resulted in massive displacement of peoples, migration, and cross-cultural encounters and exchange. Then the eighteenth and nineteenth centuries brought further revolutions in science, philosophy, and governments. Western societies were completely transformed by new forces and processes of change, among which we should list industrialization, urbanization, economic specialization, and political "liberalization." By the mid-twentieth century, the modern states of the postcolonial order had undergone a century of dramatic social upheaval. World-spanning wars and new systems of international cooperation had resulted in the creation of the global financial and political order that we see today, a world transformed by innovations in transportation, communication, international trade, and new patterns of immigration. These forces have increased the cultural diversity of many societies.

In 1789, the English colonists who established the United States of America by revolution adopted a constitutional amendment prohibiting legislative interference in the "establishment" or "free exercise" of "religion." This policy was also adopted at the level of the States; in 1833, Massachusetts became the last of the American States to disestablish its official church. In America, institutional forms that could claim the status of "religion" were not only protected from state regulation, they enjoyed a privileged legal status as a matter of individual "rights." It is widely recognized by historians of religion that "religious liberty" in America facilitated the emergence of a wild, pluralistic landscape of new churches and religious movements. Following the removal of the established churches, a social movement usually referred to as "the second great awakening" brought a twentyfold expansion in the number of working ministers and an eightfold increase in church membership during the years 1815–48 (Hatch 1989; Howe 2007). While this period of expansion in "religion" mainly had the effect of creating an "evangelical consensus" among Americans (putting Protestant Christianity firmly into the position of cultural dominance over America that it still enjoys today), it also led to the proliferation of a variety of alternative religious forms. A large number of these ultimately came to be labeled as "cults" by participants in the dominant culture (this includes Christian Science, Church of the Latter-Day Saints aka the Mormons, Millerites aka Adventists, and many others).

Innovation continued apace into the twentieth century, as the American "marketplace" of options was continuously transformed by the ferment created in the context of mass communication, international trade, urbanization, and immigration. This cultural diversity that has emerged in American cities brought further waves of variety and novelty in religion, and the "secular" American system, which treats "religion" as a matter of individual right, has helped to ensure that novel groups and movements could continuously form.

The modern states that have emerged during the past century and a half are sometimes described as multicultural or "globalized." In our contemporary "postcolonial" situation, critics speak of "the porous pluralism of late modernity" (Hefner 1998), in which people find themselves in "culturally heterogeneous" societies (Hall 2019 [2000]). Arguably, it is even possible to speak today of the "transcultural individual" (Epstein 2009).

Contemporary American uses of the word "cult" have emerged in this context. In a political context where "religious liberty" makes governmental regulation of religious institutions more difficult, dominant institutions have reinforced their dominance by promoting the classification of small, nondominant groups as "cults." The word serves as a specialized tool for reinforcing boundaries between what is deemed normative, and what "deviant," in matters of religion, and the boundary between "deviant" and "normal" religiosity is drawn based on a conceptual scheme inherited from the "evangelical consensus" of earlier times.

As Megan Goodwin has written, in explaining the violence done by the term "cult" and also by the idea that "cults are not real religions":

> America has been, since its inception, a space that both fosters and punishes radical religious innovation—we have enshrined certain religious protections in our founding documents, but disincentivize any religious difference deemed too far from the (predominantly white Christian) mainstream. Groups too far beyond the pale of acceptable American religiosity are "cults." (Goodwin 2018, 238)

The Twentieth-Century Anti-Cult Movement in the United States

In the United States, popular concern about "cults" peaked in the mid- to late twentieth century. This era of concern is not intelligible apart from its social contexts, including the rise of the "counterculture" and the "sexual revolution" of the 1960s; the associated movement of popular opposition to America's involvement in the postcolonial wars of Southeast Asia; the decline in participation in the "mainline" Christian churches; the rise of nondenominational fundamentalist Christianity; and the increasingly widespread public interest in and awareness of non-Christian traditions. In this context of cultural change and ferment, there emerged an "anti-cult" movement that ended up reaching and influencing a broad popular audience.

Arguably, evangelical Christian apologists kicked off the mid-twentieth century anti-cult movement. Baptist theologian Walter R. Martin presented the study of "cults" as a defense of orthodox Christianity (Martin 1955). One of the most influential books from the Christian counter-cult movement was Martin's 1965 treatise *The Kingdom of the Cults: An Analysis of Major Cult Systems in the Present Christian Era*; this book remains in print and has gone through six updated editions. The most recent edition (2003) lists the now disgraced evangelical apologist Ravi Zacharias as a coauthor. If it was not already so used prior to the 1950s, after this period "cult" became a potent insider's term used by American evangelicals.

The late twentieth century saw the creation of numerous "anti-cult" organizations, many of which had ties to the evangelical community. The controversial activist Ted Patrick helped to found two of the most prominent groups: The Parents' Committee to Free Our Children from the Children of God (FREECOG) (founded in 1971) and the Citizen's Freedom Foundation (founded in 1974). These later merged into the Cult Awareness Network (CAN) (founded in 1978). Also important was the American Family Foundation (AFF) (founded in 1979), which later changed its name to the International Cultic Studies Association (ICSA) (in 2004); the AFF/ICSA has published a series of journals under various names: *Cult Observer, Cultic Studies Journal, Cultic Studies Review,* and *International Journal of Cultic Studies.*

CAN founder Ted Patrick promoted the then-popular idea that cult members had suffered "brainwashing" (see Lifton 1961). He coined the term "deprogramming" as a name for the nonvoluntary process he used to convince adherents to abandon their chosen communities (these deprogramming institutions were in many ways similar to our present-day gay deconversion therapy programs). In 1976, Patrick published a book detailing his mission and methods, *Let Our Children Go!* (The cover of this book bore the subtitle "by the man who rescues brainwashed American youth from sinister 'religious' cults.") It is worth noting that in 1980, Patrick was convicted of kidnapping in connection with his "deprogramming" activities and sentenced to five years of probation.

Over the nearly two decades of its existence, CAN became a major source of "information" about "cults," deeply shaping public perceptions of minority religious groups in America. (In an ironic twist, after lawsuits from the allegedly "cultic" Church of Scientology forced CAN into bankruptcy, the CAN name and assets were acquired by a prominent Scientologist in 1997.) Yet the demise of CAN has not brought anti-cult activism to an end in America. Anti-cult activism persists, often in the form of evangelical Christian ministries which focus on debunking "false" religions.

The Sociological Literature on Cults

The anti-cult movement of the late twentieth century found some support from the work of academic sociologists of religion, who, though they did not organize specifically around an anti-cult agenda, nevertheless provided a seemingly scientific foundation for classifying certain groups as "cults."

In the mid-twentieth century, sociological research on religion remained beholden to a "church-sect" typology that was rooted in the sociological research of Max Weber and Ernst Troelsch. The "church-sect typology" had been developed mainly in an effort to explain institutional variation and complexity in the Christian tradition of Europe and America. It had only secondarily been used cross-culturally to model institutional forms in non-Christian contexts. In an influential 1963 article, the American sociologist Benton Johnson proposed a revision of the typology that was meant to make it more general and universal. He proposed to define "a church [as] a religious group that accepts the social environment in which it exists" and "a sect [as] a religious group that rejects the social environment in which it exists" (Johnson 1963, 542). Interestingly, Johnson's article nowhere makes mention of the idea of "cults" as a part of the American religious scene. Johnson regarded American religion as dominated by a majority who remain involved in society-accepting "churchly" institutions, while pointing to a range of (mostly Protestant Christian) "sectarian" groups that offer society-rejecting alternatives. His interest in non-Protestant or non-Christian groups was mostly confined to the question of how to classify minority populations of Catholic and Jewish Americans according to his revised "church-sect" typology.

In an important article published in 1979 in the *Journal for the Scientific Study of Religion*, sociologists William Bainbridge and Rodney Stark proposed to further modify Johnson's reformulation of the "church-sect" typology by introducing the term "cult" as a means of refining Johnson's concept of society-rejecting "sects." Johnson had defined "sects" as religious movements that stood in a "high state of tension with their surrounding socio-cultural environment"; now Bainbridge and Stark proposed to distinguish between "two kinds" of such "deviant" groups (Stark and Bainbridge 1979, 124). The term "sect," in keeping with traditional uses of the term, was to be used for movements that were "schismatic" or "offshoots," of established traditions. In contrast, they proposed, "cult" would be used to designate groups based on "cultural *innovation*" or "cultural *importation*" (emphasis original). Hence, they opined, "[t]he cult may represent an alien (external) religion, or it may have originated in the host society—but through innovation, not fission" (Stark and Bainbridge 1979, 125). And again: "sects are breeds of a common species; cults are a different species and occur by mutation and migration" (Stark and Bainbridge 1979, 126). In the same year, Stark and Bainbridge, along with coauthor Daniel Boyle, also published a survey in which they examined "the geographic distribution of American cults," drawing directly on their argument that cults be defined as distinctly novel religious movements. They found that the majority of American cults and cultists were located in California and the American West (Stark, Bainbridge, and Doyle 1979).

Interestingly, in a closely related article published in 1980, which also works with updating Johnson's "church-sect" typology, Bainbridge and Stark do not use the language of "cults" at all. In this article, they proposed ways to quantify social "tension" and so to provide a scale on which we can measure "deviant subculture." In the process, they identify as *sects* "such groups as the Moonies, the Hare Krishnas, the Love Family, the Children of

God, and the New Testament Missionary Fellowship," noting that these sects met sometimes violent social opposition—they cited Patrick's 1976 book on "deprogramming" cult members!—and suggesting that this was one manifestation of the "tension" between "sects" and society they sought to measure (Stark and Bainbridge 1980, 106).

These sociological types termed "church," "sect," and "cult" were further rationalized in Bainbridge and Stark's 1987 book *A Theory of Religion*, which defines *sect* as "a deviant religious organization with traditional beliefs and practices" and *cult* as "a deviant religious organization with novel beliefs and practices" (Stark and Bainbridge 1987, 124).

The language Stark and Bainbridge used to describe "cults" in 1979 appears startling by today's academic standards. Their model of "cults" mainly offers a not very helpful insight that social tensions can result from the introduction of novel forms into systems dominated by a particular tradition. But by characterizing certain movements as "mutations," "alien" in origin, or the result of "migrations," or "importation," Bainbridge and Stark appear to center and authorize the perspective of the dominant religious culture (White, European, Protestant, and Christian), which viewed itself as facing an external threat. This "sociology" is not the disinterested gaze of objective science. It just puts a scientific gloss on nativist impulses. Over forty years later, we see that, instead of providing us with a useful theory of "cults," Bainbridge and Stark provide us with insight into the social function of the term "cult" in late twentieth-century America.

From the same period (the 1960s and 1970s), there are in fact numerous examples of sociological literature dealing with "cults." Much of this literature shows that sociologists had largely failed to reach a consensus on how best to employ the term, and virtually all of it seems outdated from a contemporary perspective (see, e.g., Campbell 1978, and his bibliography).

The Future of the Word "Cult"

At present, the problematic word "cult" continues to be used with a wide currency. A google search conducted in early 2022 turned up more than 2.6 *billion* web pages using the term. It seems safe to predict that people will continue to disparage minority religious movements (and their social opponents) by tarring them with the term. Although there are some social psychologists who continue to find utility in speaking of "cults" and their characteristics (see, e.g., Lifton 2019 and cf. Singer 2003), today most contemporary scholars of religion actively discourage using the word. To borrow a term from Catherine Wessinger, we ought to avoid participating in "culting" religious minorities

(Wessinger 2009, also Wessinger 2013). Megan Goodwin publicly denounces the use of the word "cult" (even though she teaches a course called "Cults"). Revealing that she "hate[s] this word," she offers the well-stated observation that "the word 'cult' gets used to mark certain groups as legitimate targets of state surveillance and violence" (Goodwin 2020).

In a recently published book, Russell McCutcheon and Aaron Hughes suggest that the word "should probably be retired" from use in academic Religious Studies, to be henceforth treated as "an artifact from an earlier time . . . indicative of earlier interests and assumptions" (Hughes and McCutcheon 2022, 58). The scholar of religion, they suggest, should attend to how the word continues to function as a boundary-setting mechanism in our society.

Over the past several decades, many scholars of religion, including sociologists, have come to prefer the phrase "new religious movements" (NRMs) as a way of referring to groups often otherwise labeled "cults." The journal *Nova Religio*, dedicated to "emergent and alternative religious movements" is currently into its twenty-fifth volume. But while the NRM label has been shown to be received with less prejudice by members of the general public (Olson 2006) even this phrase has certain acknowledged problems, including the fact that many supposedly novel religious groups appear to be based on at least some ancient traditions, and are "new" only from the perspective of the dominant tradition. Rebecca Moore offers the opinion that perhaps groups of interest should not be classified at all, but referred to instead by their chosen names. For her concern she (along with many other scholars of NRMs) has been labeled a "cult apologist" by the anti-cult activist community (for a discussion of this, see Moore 2018). Goodwin often uses the term "minority religions" in her work.

Notes

Chapter 1

1 A nonexhaustive list of resources discussing this topic include Finbarr Curtis' *The Production of American Religious Freedom* (2016), Tracy Fessenden's *Culture and Redemption* (2011), Charles McCrary's *Sincerely Held* (2022), Catherine Albanese's *America: Religions and Religion* (2013), David Sehat's *The Myth of American Religious Freedom* (2011), and Winnifred Fallers Sullivan's *The Impossibility of Religious Freedom* (2005).

Chapter 2

1 In this chapter, we center our discussion of religious freedom on the United States and the First Amendment of the US constitution. There is, of course, a wide selection of scholarship on the topic in other international contexts. For example, we suggest the edited (Sullivan et al.) collection *Politics of Religious Freedom* (2015) and *Beyond Religious Freedom: The New Global Politics of Religion* (2015) by Elizabeth Shakman Hurd for international and comparative analyses on religious freedom. Other works, like *Faking Liberties: Religious Freedom in American-Occupied Japan* (2019) by Jolyon Baraka Thomas and *Why the French Don't Like Headscarves: Islam, the State, and Public Space* (2007) by John Bowen, provide nation-specific examples of religious freedom in non-US contexts.

2 She was a member of an IRS-recognized religion, The Satanic Temple, which has as one of its tenets the right to control one's body (see The Satanic Temple no date).

3 In *The Political Origins of Religious Liberty* (2007), Anthony Gill argues that these clusters of decisions by a government are not based on the open-minded ideals we like to claim, rather they are based on governments weighing outcomes and making rational choices in the interest of state stability.

4 *The Impossibility of Religious Freedom* (2005) by Winnifred Fallers Sullivan is one of the most popular contemporary works on religious freedom, and, as a result, the word "impossible" is often used when talking about guaranteeing religious freedom. Stanley Fish also uses the word in his article, "Mission Impossible: Settling the Just Bound between Church and State" (1997).

5 Leslie Dorrough Smith' debunking of the cliché "Religion Concerns the Transcendent" in *Stereotyping Religion* (2017) cites Lincoln's *Holy Terrors* (2003), suggesting that the vagueness and pliability of religious talk (about "the sacred" for example) serves useful for justifying a wide range of endeavors precisely because of the ways it does not define the subject but is, instead, a discourse that can reframe anything as sacred.

6 There is Jefferson's famous "wall of separation" and Madison was the author of the First Amendment but, as pointed out by a reviewer, William Penn's earlier creative and strategic approach of religious freedom is often overlooked. Penn appealed to the English Crown in 1675 for religious liberty and religious tolerance as beneficial to commerce, prosperity, and happiness. See Anthony Gill (2007), pages 98–99.

7 Notice how the term "sacrifice" indicates a claim, bias, or judgment that the thing done is considered religious or even irrational. Also, although this particular case was about the killing of chickens, other domesticated livestock can be involved, such as goats.

8 SCOTUS' ruling in the Hialeah case was a rejection of the ruling made in *Reynolds v. United States* (1879) that ruled against a member of the Church of Jesus Christ of Latter-day Saints' (LDS) claim to religious freedom to receive exemption from laws prohibiting plural marriages.

9 While Hobby Lobby is often referenced as the sole plaintiff, the case included another family-held retail business with owners from a different Protestant denomination, Conestoga Wood (a Mennonite-owned business).

Chapter 4

1 The discussion of Schleiermacher and Otto closely follows Craig Martin's argument in "Experience" (see Martin 2016).

Chapter 5

1 Part of this section is published elsewhere in Ting Guo, "Lost in Žižek, Redeemed in Cloud Atlas: Buddhism and Other Tales of 'Asian Religions' in Western Cinema and Affective Circulation" (Guo 2022).

2 Of course, Žižek might be perfectly aware that his interpretation of Buddhism may be essentialist and subject to decolonial critiques and yet chooses to discuss Buddhism in this way precisely because it is the dominant interpretation of Buddhism in the West.

3 The PRC nonetheless recognizes five religions: Buddhism, Daoism, Islam, Catholicism, and Protestantism, though only to be practiced under state-sanctioned institutions and frameworks.

4 Yang broadened Joachim Wach's notion of "natural groups" and "specifically religious" into institutional religion and diffused religion, with reference to Durkheim's take on "diffused form of religion" in *Elementary Forms of the Religious Life* (1915) and *Professional Ethics and Civic Morals* (1957). See C. K. Yang, *Religion in Chinese Society* (1961).

5 This paragraph also appears in Guo forthcoming.

Chapter 6

1 There is a fascinating parallel here with the way that colonialism placed humans into a tripartite "racial" classification according to their supposed position on the evolutionary scale between irrational animals and (supposedly) fully rational Europeans, with "Indians" ranking above "Negroes" (Wynter 2003, 300–2).

2 Even the scholarly tendency to describe them as New Religious Movements (NRMs) still makes this implicit distinction. Not only does it keep the descriptor "New," implying that this is a difference so fundamental that they require their own subcategory, but the term "religious movements" suggests that they might be *like* religions but not sufficiently like them to actually *grant them* that name.

Bibliography

Chapter 1

Albanese, Catherine L. (2013). *America: Religions and Religion*, 5th edition, Boston, MA: Wadsworth.

Bell, Matthew (2019). "The Satanic Temple Gets Religion." *The World*. Available at https://theworld.org/stories/2019-05-06/satanic-temple-gets-religious.

Braun, Willi (2000). "Religion." In R. T. McCutcheon and Willi Braun (eds.), *The Guide to the Study of Religion*, 3–20, New York, NY: T&T Clark.

Burwell v. Hobby Lobby Stores, Inc., 573 U.S. 682 (2014).

Curtis, Finbarr (2016). *The Production of American Religious Freedom*, New York: New York University Press.

Dickson, EJ (2019). "The IRS Officially Recognizes the Satanic Temple as a Church." *Rolling Stone*. Available at https://www.rollingstone.com/culture/culture-news/irs-satanic-temple-church-tax-exempt-826931/.

Employment Division, Department of Human Services of Oregon v. Smith, 494 U.S. 872 (1990).

Fessenden, Tracy (2005). "The Nineteenth Century Bible Wars and the Separation of Church and State." *Church History* 74 (4): 784–811.

Fessenden, Tracy (2011). *Culture and Redemption: Religion, the Secular, and American Literature*, Princeton, NJ: Princeton University Press.

Laycock, Joseph P. (2020). *Speak of the Devil: How The Satanic Temple Is Changing the Way We Talk about Religion*, New York, NY: Oxford University Press.

Martin, Craig (2010). *Masking Hegemony: A Genealogy of Liberalism, Religion and the Private Sphere*, New York: Routledge.

Martin, Craig (2022). *Discourse and Ideology: A Critique of the Study of Culture*, New York: Bloomsbury.

McCrary, Charles (2022). *Sincerely Held: American Secularism and Its Believers*, Chicago, IL: University of Chicago Press.

Nongbri, Brent (2013). *Before Religion: A History of a Modern Concept*, New Haven, CT: Yale University Press.

Nye, Malory (2004). *Religion: The Basics*, New York: Routledge.

Otto, Rudolf (1958). *The Idea of the Holy*, New York: Oxford University Press.

Ramey, Steven W. (2017). "Do All Religious Adherents Believe in the Concept of a Higher Power?" In A. W. Hughes and R. T. McCutcheon (eds.), *Religion in 5 Minutes*, 30–3, Bristol, CT: Equinox Publishing.

Reynolds v. United States, 98 U.S. 145 (1878).

Sehat, David (2011). *The Myth of American Religious Freedom*, New York: Oxford University Press.

Sullivan, Winnifred F. (2005). *The Impossibility of Religious Freedom*, Princeton, NJ: Princeton University Press.

Walsh, Robyn F. (2017). "Religion Is a Private Matter." In B. Stoddard and C. Martin (eds.), *Stereotyping Religion: Critiquing Clichés*, 69–82, New York: Bloomsbury.

Weiner, Isaac (2017). "The Corporately Produced Conscience: Emergency Contraception and the Politics of Workplace Accommodations." *Journal of the American Academy of Religion* 85 (1): 31–63.

Chapter 2

Bowen, John R. (2007). *Why the French Don't Like Headscarves: Islam, the State, and Public Space*, Princeton, NJ: Princeton University Press.

Crosson, J. Brent (2020). *Experiments with Power: Obeah and the Remaking of Religion*, Chicago, IL: University of Chicago Press.

Fish, Stanley (1997). "Mission Impossible: Settling the Just Bound between Church and State." *Columbia Law Review* 97 (8): 2255–333.

Gill, Anthony (2007). *The Political Origins of Religious Liberty*, Cambridge: Cambridge University Press.

Hurd, Elizabeth Shakman (2015). *Beyond Religious Freedom: The New Global Politics of Religion*, Princeton, NJ: Princeton University Press.

Lofton, Kathryn (2017). *Consuming Religion*, Chicago, IL: University of Chicago Press.

O'Brien, David M. (2004). *Animal Sacrifice and Religious Freedom: Church of the Lukumi Babalu Aye v. City of Hialeah*, Lawrence: University Press of Kansas.

Satanic Temple, The. (n.d). "About Us." *Thesatanictemple.com*. Available at https://thesatanictemple.com/pages/about-us

Sullivan, Winnifred Fallers (2005). *The Impossibility of Religious Freedom*, Princeton, NJ: Princeton University Press.

Sullivan, Winnifred Fallers (2020). *Church State Corporation: Construing Religion in US Law*, Chicago, IL: University of Chicago Press.

Sullivan, Winnifred Fallers, et al. (2015). *Politics of Religious Freedom*, Chicago, IL: University of Chicago Press.

Thomas, Jolyon Baraka (2019). *Faking Liberties: Religious Freedom in American-Occupied Japan*, Chicago, IL: University of Chicago Press.

Urban, Hugh (2015). *New Age, Neopagan, and New Religious Movements: Alternative Spirituality in Contemporary America*, Berkeley: University of California Press.

Chapter 3

American Humanist Association (2021). "American Humanist Association Board Statement Withdrawing Honor from Richard Dawkins." *American Humanist Association*. Available at https://americanhumanist.org/news/american

-humanist-association-board-statement-withdrawing-honor-from-richard
-dawkins/#:~:text=His%20subsequent%20attempts%20at%20clarification
,Humanist%20of%20the%20Year%20award.

Amis, Martin (2002). "The Voice of the Lonely Crowd." *Guardian*. Available at
https://www.theguardian.com/books/2002/jun/01/philosophy.society.

BBC (2017). "Farron Quits as Lib Dem Leader Over Clash Between Faith and
Politics." *BBC News*. Available at https://www.bbc.com/news/uk-politics
-40281300.

Beardsley, Christina and Michelle O'Brian, eds. (2016). *This Is My Body: Hearing
the Theology of Transgender Christians*, London: Darton, Longman, and Todd
Ltd.

Beattie, Tina (2007). *The New Atheists: The Twilight of Reason and the War on
Religion*, London: Darton, Longman and Todd.

Boswell, John (1980). *Christianity, Social Tolerance, and Homosexuality: Gay
People in Western Europe from the Beginning of the Christian Era to the
Fourteenth Century*, Chicago, IL: University of Chicago Press.

Brand, Russell (2014). *Revolution*, London: Century.

Butler, Judith (1990). *Gender Trouble: Feminism and the Subversion of Identity*,
New York: Routledge.

Channel 4 (2015). "Tim Farron Asked Three Times if Gay Sex is a Sin." *4 News*.
Available at https://www.channel4.com/news/tim-farron-asked-three-times-if
-gay-sex-is-a-sin.

Clements, Ben (2015). *Religion and Public Opinion in Britain: Continuity and
Change*, Basingstoke: Palgrave.

Clements, Ben (2017). "Attitudes Towards Gay Rights." *British Religion in
Numbers*. Available at http://www.brin.ac.uk/figures/attitudes-towards-gay
-rights/.

Cohen, Nick (2014). "Revolution by Russell Brand Review – The Barmy Redo of a
Beverly Hills Buddhist." *Observer*. Available at https://www.theguardian.com/
books/2014/oct/27/revolution-review-russell-brand-beverly-hills-buddhist.

Crossley, James (2016 [2014]). *Harnessing Chaos: The Bible in English Political
Discourse Since 1968*, revised edition, London: Bloomsbury/T&T Clark.

Crossley, James (2018). *Cults, Martyrs, and Good Samaritans: Religion in
Contemporary English Political Discourse*, London: Pluto.

Dawkins, Richard (2001). "Religion's Misguided Missiles." *Guardian*. Available at
https://www.theguardian.com/world/2001/sep/15/september11.politicsphiloso
phyandsociety1.

Dawkins, Richard (2006). *The God Delusion*, London: Bantam Press.

Eagleton, Terry (2009). *Reason, Faith, and Revolution: Reflections on the God
Debate*, New Haven and London: Yale University Press.

Farron, Tim (2017). "Why I had to Choose Between my Christianity or Leading
the Lib Dems." *Spectator*. Available at https://www.spectator.co.uk/article/tim
-farron-why-i-had-to-choose-between-my-christianity-or-leading-the-lib-dems.

Foucault, Michel (1979). *The History of Sexuality. Volume 1: An Introduction*,
London: Allen Lane.

Foucault, Michel (1985). *The History of Sexuality. Volume 2: The Use of Pleasure*,
New York: Pantheon Books.

Foucault, Michel (1986). *The History of Sexuality. Volume 3: The Care of the Self*,
New York: Pantheon.

Gander, Kashmiri (2017). "Muslim, Jews and Christians on Being LGBT and Believing in God." *Independent*. Available at https://www.independent .co.uk/life-style/love-sex/lgbt-muslims-christians-jews-stonewall-beliefs-god-faith-role-models-lifestyle-gay-lesbians-trans-bisexual-a7666846 .html.

Halperin, David M. (1990). *One Hundred Years of Homosexuality: And Other Essays on Greek Love*, New York: Routledge.

Halperin, David M. (2002). *How to Do the History of Homosexuality*, Chicago, IL: University of Chicago Press.

Hansard (2013). "Marriage (Same Sex Couples) Bill." *Hansard: Commons Debates*: 125–230.

Hari, Johann (2009). "A Civil Partnership: Interview with Tony Blair." *Attitude*: 50–2.

Harris, Sam (2004). *The End of Faith: Religion, Terror, and the Future of Reason*, London: Simon & Schuster.

Hattenstone, Simon (2015). "The Cult of Jeremy Corbyn, the Great Silverback Mouse." *Guardian*. Available at https://www.theguardian.com/politics/2015/sep /29/jeremy-corbyn-labour-conference-great-silverback-mouse.

Hinchy, Jessica B. (2022). "Hijras and South Asian Historiography." *History Compass* 20 (2): 1–13.

Janssen, Dirk-Jan and Peer Scheepers (2018). "How Religiosity Shapes Rejection of Homosexuality Across the Globe." *Journal of Homosexuality* 66 (14): 1974–2001.

Kessler, Gwynn (2007). "Bodies in Motion: Preliminary Notes on Queer Theory and Rabbinic Literature." In Todd Penner and Caroline vander Stichele (eds.), *Mapping Gender in Ancient Religious Discourses*, 389–409, Leiden: Brill.

McAnulla, Stuart, Steven Kettell, and Marcus Schulzke (2018). *The Politics of New Atheism*, New York: Routledge.

O'Connor, J. and R. Cohen, eds. (2015). *Christian Role Models for LGBT Equality*, London: Stonewall.

O'Donnell, Paul (2021). "Lutherans Elect Megan Rohrer First Transgender Bishop." *Religion News Service*. Available at https://religionnews.com/2021/05 /09/lutherans-elect-megan-rohrer-first-transgender-bishop/.

Puar, Jasbir K. (2007). *Terrorist Assemblages: Homonationalism in Queer Times*, Durham, NC: Duke University Press.

Sedgwick, Eve K. (1990). *Epistemology of the Closet*, Berkeley: University of California Press.

Schafer, Mac (2021). "*Euphoria* Star Hunter Schafer's Dad Mac on Why His Faith Calls Him to Support Trans Equality." *People*. Available at https://people.com/ human-interest/euphoria-star-hunter-schafer-dad-mac-schafer-speaks-out-faith -trans-equality/.

Wakefield, Lily (2021). "Joe Biden's Inaugural Prayer Service was "the Most LGBT-Inclusive in History" with Blessing for Trans and Gay People." *Pink News*. Available at https://www.pinknews.co.uk/2021/01/21/inaugural-prayer -service-joe-biden-lgbt-faith-leaders-sermon-prayer/.

Zwilling, Leonard and Michael J. Sweet (1996). "'Like a City Ablaze': The Third Sex and the Creation of Sexuality in Jain Religious Literature." *Journal of the History of Sexuality* 6 (3): 359–84.

Chapter 4

Carrette, Jeremy and Richard King (2005). *Selling Spirituality: The Silent Takeover of Religion*, London: Routledge.

King, Richard (1999). *Orientalism and Religion: Postcolonial Theory, India and "The Mystic East,"'* London: Routledge.

Lepherd, Laurence (2014). "Spirituality: Everyone Has It, but What Is It?." *International Journal of Nursing Practice* 21 (5): 566–74.

Lipka, Michael and Claire Gecewicz (2017). "More Americans Now Say They're Spiritual But Not Religious." *Pew Research Center.* Available at https://www.pewresearch.org/fact-tank/2017/09/06/more-americans-now-say-theyre-spiritual-but-not-religious/.

Martin, Craig (2014). *Capitalizing Religion: Ideology and the Opiate of the Bourgeoisie*, London: Bloomsbury Publishing.

Martin, Craig (2016). "Experience." In Michael Stausberg and Steven Engler (eds.), *The Oxford Handbook of the Study of Religion*, 525–40, Oxford: Oxford University Press.

Miller, Lisa, Iris M Balodis, Clayton H. McClintock, Jiansong Xu, Cheryl M Lacadie, Rajita Sinha, and Marc N. Potenza (2019). "Neural Correlates of Personalized Spiritual Experiences." *Cerebral Cortex* 29 (6): 2331–8.

Otto, Rudolf (1958 [1917]). *The Idea of the Holy*, translated by John W. Harvey, Oxford: Oxford University Press.

Peng-Keller, S. (2019). "Genealogies of Spirituality: An Historical Analysis of a Travelling Term." *Journal for the Study of Spirituality* 9 (2): 86–98.

Said, Edward (1978). *Orientalism*, New York: Pantheon Books.

Schleiermacher, Friedrich (1996 [1799]). *On Religion: Speeches to its Cultured Despisers*, translated by Richard Crouter, Cambridge: Cambridge University Press.

Schmidt, Leigh E. (2012 [2005]). *Restless Souls: The Making of American Spirituality*, Berkeley: University of California Press.

Whitman, Walt (1973). "Democratic Vistas." In M. V. Doren (ed.), *The Portable Walt Whitman*, New York: Viking Penguin, 317–84.

Chapter 5

No author. (2014). "Spiritual Capitalism? Global Fitness Brand Lululemon Comes to London." *Evening Standard.* Available at https://www.standard.co.uk/lifestyle/london-life/spiritual-capitalism-global-fitness-brand-lululemon-comes-to-london-9232686.html.

No author (2022). "lululemon and Yoga." *lululemon.com.* Available at https://www.lululemon.com.hk/en-hk/company/lululemon-and-yoga/lululemon-yoga.html.

Abu-Lughod, L. (2013). *Do Muslim Women Need Saving?*, Cambridge, MA: Harvard University Press.

Arjana, Sophia R. (2020). *Buying Buddha, Selling Rumi: Orientalism and the Mystical Marketplace*, London: Oneworld Academic.

Bell, Daniel (2014). "Reconciling Confucianism and Nationalism." *Journal of Chinese Philosophy* 41 (1–2): 33–54.

Bird, Lauren (2014). "Ancient Wisdom, Modern Bodies: Hybrid Authenticity in the Space of Modern Yoga." Masters thesis, Concordia University.

Campbell, Colin (2001). "A New Age Theodicy for a New Age." In P. Heelas, D. Martin, and L. Woodhead (eds.), *Peter Berger and the Study of Religion*, 73–84, York: Routledge.

Chau, Adam Y. (2005). *Miraculous Response: Doing Popular Religion in Contemporary China*, Stanford: Stanford University Press.

Chow, Rey (1995). "Between Colonizer and Colonizer: Self-Creation of a Hong Kong Postcoloniality in the 90s" 殖民者與殖民者之間：九十年代香港的後殖民自創, *Today* 今天 28: 185–206.

Faber, MEI D. (1996). *New Age Thinking: A Psychoanalytic Critique*, Ottawa: University of Ottawa.

Frayling, C. (2014). *The Yellow Peril: Dr Fu Manchu & the Rise of Chinaphobia*, London: Thames & Hudson.

Guo, Ting (2021). "'So Many Mothers, So Little Love': Discourse of Motherly Love and Parental Governance in 2019 Hong Kong Protests." *Method and Theory in the Study of Religion* 34 (1–2): 3–24.

Guo, Ting (2022). "Lost in Žižek, Redeemed in Cloud Atlas: Buddhism and Other Tales of 'Asian Religions' and Affective Circulation." In T. Eaghll and R. King (eds.), *Representing Religion in Film*, 101–16, London: Bloomsbury.

Guo, Ting (forthcoming). "Beyond Sing Hallelujah to the Lord: Diffused Religion and Religious Co-Optations through Hong Kong Protests." *Journal of American Academy of Religion*.

Harrison, Henrietta (2013). *The Missionary's Curse and Other Tales from a Chinese Catholic Village*, Berkeley: University of California Press.

Heelas, Paul (1996). *The New Age Movement*, Oxford: Blackwell Publishers.

Heelas, Paul and Linda Woodhead (2005). *The Spiritual Revolution: Why Religion Is Giving Way to Spirituality*, London: Wiley-Blackwell.

Hsia, Florence C. (2009). *Sojourners in a Strange Land: Jesuits and Their Scientific Missions in Late Imperial China*, Chicago, IL: University of Chicago Press.

Huang, Julia C. (2009). *Charisma and Compassion: Cheng Yen and the Buddhist Tzu Chi Movement*, Cambridge, MA: Harvard University Press.

Jain, Andrea R. (2020). *Peace Love Yoga: The Politics of Global Spirituality*, Oxford: Oxford University Press.

Kao, Chen-yang (2009). "The Cultural Revolution and the Emergence of Pentecostal-Style Protestantism in China." *Journal of Contemporary Religion* 24 (2): 171–88.

Keevak, M. (2011). *Becoming Yellow: A Short History of Racial Thinking*, Princeton, NJ: Princeton University Press.

King, Richard (1999). *Orientalism and Religion: Post-Colonial Theory, India and "The Mystic East."* New York: Routledge.

King, S. B. (2009). *Socially Engaged Buddhism*, Honolulu: University of Hawaii Press.

Lavrence, Christine and Kristin Lozanski (2014). "'This Is Not Your Practice Life': Lululemon and the Neoliberal Governance of Self." *The Canadian Review of Sociology* 51 (1): 76–94.

Lee, C. and L. Han (2015). "Recycling Bodhisattva: The Tzu-Chi Movement's Response to Global Climate Change." *Social Compass* 62 (3): 311–25.

Lee, Chengpang and Ling Han (2016). "Mothers and Moral Activists: Two Models of Women's Social Engagement in Contemporary Taiwanese

Buddhism." *Nova Religio: The Journal of Alternative and Emergent Religions* 19 (3): 54–77.

Lee, Chengpang and Ling Han (2021). "Taiwanese Buddhism and Environmentalism: A Mixed Method Study." *Review of Religion and Chinese Society* 9 (1): 1–26.

Madsen, Richard and Elijah Siegler (2011). "The Globalization of Chinese Religions and Traditions." In David A. Palmer, Glenn Shive, and Philip L. Wickeri (eds.), *Chinese Religious Life*, 227–40, Oxford: Oxford University Press.

Mahmood, Saba (2015). *The Religious Difference in a Secular Age: A Minority Report*, Princeton, NJ: Princeton University Press.

Møllgaard, Eske (2008). "Slavoj Žižek's Critique of Western Buddhism." *Contemporary Buddhism* 9 (2): 167–80.

Owen, Suzanne (2011). "The World Religions Paradigm Time for a Change." *Arts and Humanities in Higher Education* 10 (3): 253–68.

Palmer, David and Vincent Goosaert (2004). *The Religious Question of Modern China*, Durham, NC: Duke University Press.

Putcha, Rumya S. (2020). "Yoga and White Public Space." *Religions* 11 (12): 669.

Said, Edward (2014). *Orientalism*, New York: Vintage Books.

Schluessel, Eric (2020). *Land of Strangers: The Civilizing Project in Qing Central Asia*, New York: Columbia University Press.

Skirbekk, Vegard, Éric C. Malenfant, Stuart Basten, and Martin Stonawski (2012). "The Religious Composition of the Chinese Diaspora, Focusing on Canada." *Journal for the Scientific Study of Religion* 51 (1): 173–83.

Suh, Sharon A. (2015). *Silver Screen Buddha: Buddhism in Asian and Western Film*, New York: Bloomsbury Academic.

Xi, Lian (2013). "'Cultural Christians' and the Search for Civil Society in Contemporary China." *The Chinese Historical Review* 20 (1): 70–87.

Yang, CK (2020 [1961]). *Religion in Chinese Society: A Study of Contemporary Social Functions of Religion and Some of Their Historical Factors*, Berkeley: University of California Press.

Yao, Yu-Shuang (2012). *Taiwan's Tzu Chi as Engaged Buddhism: Origins, Organization, Appeal and Social Impact*, Leiden: Brill.

Žižek, Slavoj (2001). "From Western Marxism to Western Buddhism: The Taoist Ethic and the Spirit of Global Capitalism." *Cabinet Magazine*. Available at https://www.cabinetmagazine.org/issues/2/zizek.php.

Žižek, Slavoj (2003). *The Puppet and the Dwarf: The Perverse Core of Christianity*, Cambridge, MA: The MIT Press.

Žižek, Slavoj (2006). "The Prospects of Radical Politics Today." In R. Butler and S. Stephens (eds.), *The Universal Exception: Selected Writings*, Volume 2, 476–89, London: Continuum.

Chapter 6

Awad, Nihad (2014). "ISIS Is Not Just Un-Islamic, It Is Anti-Islamic." *Time.com*. Available at https://time.com/3273873/stop-isis-islam/.

Chidester, David (1996). *Savage Systems: Colonialism and Comparative Religion in Southern Africa*, Charlottesville: University Press of Virginia.

Coren, Michael. (2021). "Is Belief Still Relevant in These Modern Times?" *Globe and Mail*. Available at https://www.theglobeandmail.com/opinion/article-is -belief-still-relevant-in-these-modern-times/.

Cotter, Christopher R. and David G. Robertson (2016). "Introduction: The World Religions Paradigm in Contemporary Religious Studies." In C. R. Cotter and D. Robertson (eds.), *After World Religions: Reconstructing Religious Studies*, 1–20, London: Routledge.

Greenwood, Marc. (2021). "In Rebuttal: Marc Greenwood: 'Authentic Christianity Requires Courage.'" *Sun Journal*. Available at https://www.sunjournal.com /2021/07/20/in-rebuttal-marc-greenwood-authentic-christianity-requires -courage/.

Hammer, Olav. (2001). *Claiming Knowledge: Strategies of Epistemology from Theosophy to the New Age*, Leiden: Brill.

Hobsbawm, Eric. (2015 [1983]). "Introduction: Inventing Tradition." In E. Hobsbawm and T. Ranger (eds.), *The Invention of Tradition*, 1–14, Cambridge: Cambridge University Press.

Hughes, Aaron. (2015). *Islam and the Tyranny of Authenticity: An Inquiry into Disciplinary Apologetics and Self-Deception*, Sheffield: Equinox.

Jerryson, Michael K. and Mark Juergensmeyer (2010). *Buddhist Warfare*, Oxford: Oxford University Press.

Josephson-Storm, Jason A. (2021). *Metamodernism: The Future of Theory*, Chicago, IL: University of Chicago Press.

Karapetyan, Ani (2017). "6 Reasons Why ISIS Is Not Islam." *Arabamerica.com*. Available at https://www.arabamerica.com/6-reasons-isis-not-islamic/.

Miles, Jack. (2014). "Preface." In Jack Miles, Wendy Doniger, Donald S. Lopez Jr., and James Robson (eds.), *The Norton Anthology of World Religions. Volume 1: Hinduism, Buddhism and Daoism*, xli–li, New York: W.W. Norton.

Obama, Barack (2014). "Transcript: President Obama's Speech on Combating ISIS and Terrorism." *Cnn.com*. Available at https://edition.cnn.com/2014/09/10/ politics/transcript-obama-syria-isis-speech/index.html?hpt=po_c1.

Otto, Rudolf. (1917). *Das Heilige—Über das Irrationale in der Idee des Göttlichen und sein Verhältnis zum Rationalen*, Breslau: Trewendt & Granier.

Perriello, Pat. (2017). "Pastor Peter Makes a Case for Authentic Christianity." *National Catholic Reporter Online*. Available at https://www.ncronline.org/ blogs/ncr-today/pastor-peter-makes-case-authentic-christianity.

Strong, John S. (2015). *Buddhisms: An Introduction*, London: Oneworld Publications.

Swoyer, Alex. (2021). "Supreme Court Rejects Florist's Case Against Participating in Same-Sex Wedding." *Washington Times*. Available at https://www .washingtontimes.com/news/2021/jul/2/supreme-court-rejects-florists-case -against-partic/.

Sykes, Stephen. (1971). "The Essence of Christianity." *Religious Studies* 7 (4): 291–305.

Tiele, Cornelis. Petrus. (1877). *Outlines of the History of Religion to the Spread of the Universal Religions*, translated by J. E. Carpenter, Boston: James Osgood & Co.

Townsend, Mark and Tracy McVeigh (2014). "British Muslims Unite in Fury at Isis Murder of Alan Henning." *Theguardian.com*. Available at https://www.theguardian .com/world/2014/oct/05/isis-murder-alan-henning-british-muslim-community.

van Buren, Paul Matthews. (1972). *The Edges of Language: An Essay in the Logic of a Religion*, London: SCM Press.

van der Leeuw, Gerhard. (1938). *Religion in Essence & Manifestation: A Study in Phenomenology*, translated by J. E. Turner, *London*: G. Allen & Unwin.
de Vogue, Ariane. (2018). "Supreme Court Rules for Colorado Baker in Same-Sex Wedding Cake Case." *CNN Politics*. Available at https://www.cnn.com/2018/06/04/politics/masterpiece-colorado-gay-marriage-cake-supreme-court.
Wenger, Tisa. (2009). *We Have a Religion: The 1920s Pueblo Indian Dance Controversy and American Religious Freedom*, Chapel Hill: University of North Carolina Press.
Wynter, Sylvia. (2003). "Unsettling the Coloniality of Being/Power/Truth/Freedom: Towards the Human, After Man, Its Overrepresentation—An Argument." *CR: The New Centennial Review* 3 (3): 257–337.

Chapter 7

Brooke, John Hedley. (1991). *Science and Religion: Some Historical Perspectives*, Cambridge: Cambridge University Press.
Brooke, John Hedley and Ronald L. Numbers, eds. (2011). *Science and Religion Around the World*, Oxford: Oxford University Press.
Drake, Stillman. (2001). *Galileo: A Very Short Introduction*, Oxford: Oxford University Press.
Draper, John William. (2009). *History of the Conflict between Religion and Science*, Cambridge: Cambridge University Press.
Gould, Stephen Jay. (1999). *Rocks of Ages: Science and Religion in the Fullness of Life*, New York: Ballantine.
Huxley, Thomas H. (1896). "The Origin of Species." In *Collected Essays*, Volume 2, 23–80, London: MacMillan.
Jewett, Andrew. (2020). *Science Under Fire: Challenges to Scientific Authority in Modern America*, Cambridge, MA: Harvard University Press.
Newton, Isaac. (1846). *The Mathematical Principles of Natural Philosophy*, translated by A. Motte, New York: Daniel Adee.
Paley, William. (1879). *Natural Theology: Or, Evidences of the Existence and Attributes of the Deity Collected from the Appearances of Nature*, New York: Sheldon & Company.
Rubenstein, Mary-Jane. (2014). *Worlds Without End: The Many Lives of the Multiverse*, New York: Columbia University Press.
Sedgwick, Adam, John Willis Clark, and Thomas McKenny Hughes (1890). *Life and Letters of the Reverend Adam Sedgwick, Volume 2*, Cambridge: Cambridge University Press.
White, Andrew Dickson. (2009). *A History of the Warfare of Science with Theology in Christendom, Volume 1*, Cambridge: Cambridge University Press.

Chapter 8

Abu-Lughod, Lila (2015). *Do Muslim Women Need Saving?* Cambridge, MA: Harvard University Press.

Dirks, Nicholas. (2001). *Castes of Mind: Colonialism and the Making of Modern India*, Princeton, NJ: Princeton University Press.

Eck, Diana L. (2001). *A New Religious America: How a "Christian Country" Has Become the World's Most Religiously Diverse Nation*, New York: HarperSan Francisco.

Frye, Marilyn. (1983). *The Politics of Reality: Essays in Feminist Theory*, Berkeley: Crossing Press.

Jalalzai, Sajida. (2021). "Please Stop Using Islam to Critique the Abortion Ban: It Only Excuses the Very Christian, Very White Roots of Anti-Choice Movements." *Religion Dispatches*. Available at https://religiondispatches.org /please-stop-using-islam-to-critique-the-abortion-ban-it-simply-excuses-the -very-christian-very-white-roots-of-anti-choice-movements/?fbclid=IwAR0-7UZ -kZrdRmHsPwcDBcUm6f_23soaxo-YnxvCDOc-XLc8MvgPiEzV9ol.

Luckovich, Mike. (2021). "Sisterhood." *The Atlanta Journal-Constitution*. Available at https://www.ajc.com/opinion/mike-luckovich-blog/902-mike-luckovich -sisterhood/H7MAJDOCQJG2FPAPM6F2UHO3W4/.

Mahmood, Saba. (2011). *Politics of Piety: The Islamic Revival and the Feminist Subject*, Princeton, NJ: Princeton Univesity Press.

Mohanty, Chandra Talped. (2003). *Feminism Without Borders: Decolonizing Theory, Practicing Solidarity*, Durham, NC: Duke University Press.

Smith, Leslie Dorrough. (2019). *Compromising Positions: Sex Scandals, Politics, and American Christianity*, New York: Oxford University Press.

Stahler, Jeff. (2021). "Editorial Cartoon." *The Star Democrat*. Available at https:// www.stardem.com/opinion/cartoons/editorial-cartoon/image_cdaa2197-8dd7 -5f7e-9490-81899f1b9f56.html.

Sumerau, J. Edward. (2012). "'That's What a Man Is Supposed to Do': Compensatory Manhood Acts in an LGBT Christian Church." *Gender & Society* 26: 461–87.

Villareal, D. (2021). "Tucker Carlson Says 'Our Body, Our Choice' to Chelsea Clinton's Claim GOP Men Avoid Vaccine." *Newsweek*. Available at https:// www.newsweek.com/tucker-carlson-says-our-body-our-choice-chelsea-clintons -claim-gop-men-avoid-vaccine-1584069.

Chapter 9

Barrows, John Henry, ed. (1893). *The World's Parliament of Religions: An Illustrated and Popular Story of the World's First Parliament of Religions, Held in Chicago in Connection with the Columbian Exposition of 1893. 2 Volumes.* Chicago: Parliament Publishing Company.

Beaman, Lori G. (2003). "The Myth of Pluralism, Diversity, and Vigor: The Constitutional Privilege of Protestantism in the United States and Canada." *Journal for the Scientific Study of Religion* 42 (3): 311–25.

Bender, Courtney and Pamela E. Klassen, eds. (2010). *After Pluralism: Reimagining Religious Engagement*, New York: Columbia University Press.

Biden, Joseph R. (2022). "A Proclamation on Religious Freedom Day, 2022." January 14. Available at https://www.whitehouse.gov/briefing-room/ presidential-actions/2022/01/14/a-proclamation-on-religious-freedom-day-2022.

Bourne, Randolph Silliman (1964). *War and the Intellectuals; Essays, 1915–1919*, New York: Harper & Row.

Cheah, Joseph (2011). *Race and Religion in American Buddhism: White Supremacy and Immigrant Adaptation*, New York: Oxford University Press.

Corrigan, John and Lynn S. Neal (2020). *Religious Intolerance in America: A Documentary History*, 2nd edition, Chapel Hill: The University of North Carolina Press.

Druyvesteyn, Kenten (1976). *The World's Parliament of Religions*, Dissertation. University of Chicago.

Eck, Diana (2001). *A New Religious America: How a "Christian Country" Has Now Become the World's Most Religiously Diverse Nation*, San Francisco: Harper San Francisco.

Hansen, Marcus Lee (1990). "The Problem of the Third Generation Immigrant" (1937). In Peter Kivisto and Dag Blanck (eds.), *American Immigrants and Their Generations: Studies and Commentaries on the Hansen Thesis After Fifty-Years*, 191–203, Chicago: University of Illinois Press.

Herberg, Will (1960). *Protestant, Catholic, Jew: An Essay in American Religious Sociology*, Garden City, NY: Anchor Books.

Hutchinson, William (2003). *Religious Pluralism in America: The Contentious History of a Founding Ideal*, New Haven, CT: Yale University Press.

Johnson, Rossiter (1898). *History of the World's Columbian Exposition*, 4 Volumes, New York: D. Appleton and Company.

Joshi, Khyati Y. (2006). *New Roots in America's Sacred Ground: Religion, Race, and Ethnicity in Indian America*. New Brunswick, NJ: Rutgers University Press.

Kallen, Horace Meyer (1915). "Democracy Versus the Melting Pot." *The Nation* 100 (February 18, 25): 190–4, 217–20.

Kallen, Horace Meyer (1956). *Cultural Pluralism and the American Idea*, Philadelphia: University of Pennsylvania Press.

Lippy, Charles (2000). *Pluralism Comes of Age: American Religious Culture in the Twentieth Century*, Armonk, NY: M.E. Sharpe.

Machacek, David W. (2003). "The Problem of Pluralism." *Sociology of Religion* 64 (2): 145–61.

Manseau, Peter (2016). "Obama Thought he Could Unite a Religiously Divided Nation. He was Wrong." *Washington Post*, January 12.

Martin, Craig (2017). *A Critical Introduction to the Study of Religion*, 2nd edition, New York: Routledge.

Masuzawa, Tomoko (2005). *The Invention of World Religions: Or, How European Universalism Was Preserved in the Language of Pluralism*, Chicago, IL and London: University of Chicago Press.

McCutcheon, Russell (2005). *The Domestication of Dissent: Or, How to Live in a Less than Perfect Nation*, London: Equinox.

"The Most Remarkable Gathering." (1893). Napoleon, OH: Democrat Northwest, September 21.

Murphy, Tim (2005). "Notes From the Field: Religious Defamation and Radical Pluralism as Challenges to the Scholar of Religion." *Council of Societies for the Study of Religion Bulletin* 34 (4): 79–83.

Omi, Michael and Howard Winant (1994). *Racial Formation in the United States: From the 1960s to the 1990s*, 2nd edition, New York: Routledge.

Park, Robert (1950). *Race and Culture*, Glencoe, IL: Free Press.

Parliament. Available at https://parliamentofreligions.org/parliament/2021-virtual.
Porterfield, Amanda (2013). "Religious Pluralism in Religious Studies." In Charles
    L. Cohen and Ronald Numbers (eds.), *Gods in America: Religious Pluralism in
    the United States*, 21–42, New York: Oxford University Press.
Reeves Kennedy and Ruby Jo (1944). "Single or Triple Melting Pot? Intermarriage
    Trends in New Haven, 1879–1940." *American Journal of Sociology* 49: 331–9.
Roberts, Martha Smith (2013). "American Religious Pluralism in Historical
    Perspective." In Vincent Biondo and Andrew Fiala (eds.), *Civility, Religious
    Pluralism, and Education*, 88–111, New York: Routledge Press.
Rydell, Robert W. (1984). *All the World's a Fair: Visions of Empire at the American
    International Expositions, 1876–1916*, Chicago, IL: University of Chicago
    Press.
Said, Edward (1979). *Orientalism*, New York: Vintage Books.
Seager, Richard, ed. (1993). *The Dawn of Religious Pluralism: Voices from the
    World's Parliament of Religions, 1893*, La Salle, IL: Open Court Publishing
    Company.
Seager, Richard (1995). *The World's Parliament of Religions: The East/West
    Encounter, Chicago, 1893*, Bloomington and Indianapolis: Indiana University
    Press.
Takaki, Ronald (1993). *A Different Mirror: A History of Multicultural America*, New
    York: Little, Brown and Company.

Chapter 10

Allen, Elizabeth. (2017). "100 Must-Read Books about Life in Cults and
    Oppressive Religious Sects." *Book Riot*. Available at https://bookriot.com/100
    -must-read-books-about-life-in-cults/.
BBC (2015). "China Executes Two Cult Members for McDonalds Murder." *BBC
    News*, February 2.
Campbell, Bruce. (1978). "A Typology of Cults." *Sociological Analysis* 39 (3):
    228–40.
Epstein, Mikhail. (2009). "Transculture: A Broad Way between Globalism and
    Multiculturalism." *The American Journal of Economics and Sociology* 68 (1):
    327–52.
Goodwin, M. (2018). "Unpacking the Bunker: Sex, Abuse, and Apocalypticism in
    'Unbreakable Kimmy Schmidt.'" *Cross Currents* 68 (2): 237–59.
Goodwin, Megan. (2020). "Cults? Full Disclosure, Y'all: I Hate this Word."
    Medium. Available at https://medium.com/cults-sects/cults-3e19ca471a6c.
Hall, Stuart. (2019). "The Multicultural Question [2000]." In David Morley (ed.),
    Chapter 4 of Essential Essays, Vol. 2: Identity and Diaspora, 95–133, Durham,
    NC: Duke University Press.
Hatch, Nathan O. (1989). *The Democratization of American Christianity*, New
    Haven, CT: Yale University Press.
Hefner, Robert W. (1998). "Multiple Modernities: Christianity, Islam, and
    Hinduism in a Globalizing Age." *Annual Review of Anthropology* 27: 83–104.
Henry, Patrick. (1981). "'And I Don't Care What It Is': The Tradition-History of a
    Civil Religion Proof-Text." *Journal of the American Academy of Religion* 49 (1):
    35–49.

Howe, Daniel Walker (2007). *What God Hath Wrought: The Transformation of America, 1815–1848*. Oxford History of the United States, New York: Oxford University Press.

Huang, Y. T. (2010). *Charlie Chan: The Untold Story of the Honorable Detective and His Rendezvous with American History*, New York: Norton.

Hughes, Aaron and Russell McCutcheon (2022). *Religion in 50 More Words: A Redescriptive Vocabulary*, Routledge.

Itkis, Sara (2015). "Why the Midnight Madness of 'The Rocky Horror Picture Show' Still Matters 40 Years Later." *IndieWire*, August 14.

Johnson, Benton. (1963). "On Church and Sect." *American Sociological Review* 28 (4): 539–49.

Latham, Jacob. (2020). "Re-Defining Aristocratic Distinction: Christian Verse Invective, Classical Culture, and the Cult of Mater Magna in Late Antique Rome." *Memoirs of the American Academy in Rome* 65: 261–306.

Lifton, Robert Jay. (1961). *Thought Reform and the Psychology of Totalism: A Study of 'Brainwashing' in China*, New York: Norton.

Lifton, Robert Jay. (1996). *Losing Reality: On Cults, Cultism, and the Mindset of Political and Religious Zealotry*, New York: The New Press.

Lifton, Robert Jay (2019). *Losing Reality: On Cults, Cultism, and the Mindset of Political and Religious Zealotry*, The New Press.

Lincoln, Bruce. (1996). "Theses on Method." *Method and Theory in the Study of Religion* 8 (3): 225–7.

Martin, Craig. (2015). *Masking Hegemony: A Genealogy of Liberalism, Religion, and the Private Sphere*, New York: Routledge.

Martin, Walter Ralston. (1955). *The Rise of the Cults: An Introductory Guide to the Non-Christian Cults*, Grand Rapids: Zondervan.

Martin, Walter Ralston. (1965). *The Kingdom of the Cults: An Analysis of Major Cult Systems in the Present Christian Era*, Bloomington, MN: Bethany Fellowship.

Meier, Barry (2017). "Inside a Secretive Group Where Women are Branded." *The New York Times*, October 17.

Moore, Rebecca. (2018). "Cult, New Religious Movement, or Minority Religion?" *Erraticus*. Available at https://jonestown.sdsu.edu/?page_id=81676.

Mosurinjohn, Sharday (2020). "Why it's Wrong to Refer to the 'cult of Trump.'" *The Conversation*, September 1.

Moynihan, Colin (2019). "Nxivm Branding Was Scripted by Sex Cult Leader to Be 'Like a Sacrifice.'" *The New York Times*, May 26.

Murray, Julia K. (2009). "'Idols' in the Temple: Icons and the Cult of Confucius." *The Journal of Asian Studies* 68 (2): 371–411.

Olson, Paul J. (2006). "The Public Perception of 'Cults' and 'New Religious Movements.'" *Journal for the Scientific Study of Religion* 45 (1): 97–106.

OpIndia, "Jesus Christ Has Returned to Earth in Form of Chinese Woman, Claims The Church of Almighty God: Read How Banned Chinese Cult Making Inroads in India." *OpIndia*, August 26.

Peck, Cecilia, dir. (2020). *Seduced: Inside the NXIVM Cult* (Documentary Series). Produced by Lionsgate Television. Starz.

Robinson, Lisa, director. (2019). *Escaping the NXIVM Cult: A Mother's Fight to Save Her Daughter*. Television film. A&E (Lifetime) Network.

Robinson, Elizabeth and Timo Sironen (2013). "A New Inscription in Oscan from Larinum: Decisive Evidence in Favor of a Local Cult of Mars and Mater (Deum?)." *Zeitschrift für Paypyrologie und Epigraphik* 185: 251–61.

Robinson, Lisa, dir. (2021). *Escaping the NXIVM Cult: A Mother's Fight to Save Her Daughter* (film). Produced by Michael Mahoney. Lifetime.

Schilbrack, Kevin. (2013). "What *Isn't* Religion?" *The Journal of Religion* 93 (3): 291–318.

Sentinel Digital Desk (2020). "Nagaland BCC Warns against Chinese Cult Church of Almighty God." *The Sentinel,* August 23.

Sharman, Jim, dir. (1975). *The Rocky Horror Picture Show* (Film). Produced by Lou Adler and Michael White. 20th Century Fox Studios.

Singer, Margaret Thaler. (2003). *Cults in Our Midst: The Continuing Fight Against Their Hidden Menace*, San Francisco: Jossey-Bass.

Spiro, Melford E. (1966). "Religion: Problems of Definition and Explanation." In M. Banton (ed.), *Anthropological Approaches to the Study of Religion*, 85–126, New York: Tavistock Publications.

Stark, Rodney and William Sims Bainbridge (1987). *A Theory of Religion*, New York: Peter Lang.

Stark, Rodney and William Sims Bainbridge (1979). "Of Churches, Sects, and Cults: Preliminary Concepts for a Theory of Religious Movements." *Journal for the Scientific Study of Religion* 18 (2): 117–31.

Stark, Rodney and William Sims Bainbridge (1980). "Sectarian Tension." *Review of Religious Research* 22 (2): 105–24.

Stark, Rodney., William Sims Bainbridge, and D. P. Doyle (1979). "Cults of America: A Reconnaissance in Space and Time." *Sociological Analysis* 40 (4): 347–59.

Taylor, Charles. (2007). *A Secular Age*, Cambridge, MA: Harvard University Press.

Wessinger, Catherine. (2009). "Culting: From Waco to Fundamentalist Mormons." *Religion Dispatches*. Available at https://religiondispatches.org/culting-from -waco-to-fundamentalist-mormons/.

Wessinger, Catherine. (2013). "The Problem is Totalism, Not "Cults": Reflections on the Thirtieth Anniversary of Jonestown." In *Alternative Considerations of Jonestown and People's Temple*, San Diego State University. Available at https://jonestown.sdsu.edu/?page_id=31459.

Contributors

Matthew C. Baldwin, PhD, is Professor and Coordinator of the Program in Religion and Philosophy at Mars Hill University, Mars Hill, NC. Primarily interested in religious traditions of the Ancient Mediterranean World, especially early Judaism and Christianity, Baldwin also teaches and conducts research in religious studies theory and method, "world" and "American" religions, and pragmatism. He is the author of *Whose Acts of Peter? Text and Historical Context of the Actus Vercellenses* (2005).

Jacob Barrett is a doctoral student at the University of North Carolina at Chapel Hill, NC, in the Department of Religious Studies. His research interests are grounded in questions about religion and governance, more specifically looking at issues of religious freedom in the United States and how notions of "sincere belief" play out through the courts while drawing on social theory and making use of computational analysis.

James Crossley, PhD, is Professor of Bible, Society, and Politics at St. Mary's University, London, England. His research interests can be put into two broad categories: Christian origins and Judaism in the first century; and politics and religion in English political discourse. He is the author of many books, most recently *Spectres of John Ball: The "Peasants' Revolt" in English Political History, 1381–2020* (2022) and *Cults, Martyrs and Good Samaritans: Religion in Contemporary English Political Discourse* (2018).

Leslie Dorrough Smith, PhD, is Professor of Religious Studies and Director of the Women's and Gender Studies Program at Avila University, Kansas City, Missouri. She specializes in the study of American evangelicalism and gender, race, and politics. Her books include *Compromising Positions: Sex Scandals, Politics, and American Christianity* (2020) and *Righteous Rhetoric: Sex, Speech, and the Politics of Concerned Women for America* (2014).

Savannah H. Finver (she/her) is a doctoral student in the Department of Comparative Studies at the Ohio State University, Columbus, Ohio. Her interests are in modern and contemporary religion, law, and politics in the

United States, with particular attention to how legal definitions of religion impact the bodies of members of minority groups. Her dissertation research primarily focuses on how the intersection of religion and family law functions to produce and mold the bodies of children into ideal citizens of the nation.

Ting Guo, is Assistant Professor of Cultural and Religious Studies, Chinese University of Hong Kong, focusing on religion, politics, and gender in transnational Asia. She is writing her first book, *Politics of Love: Religion, Secularism, and Love as a Political Discourse in Modern China*. Her works have appeared or are forthcoming in journals including *Journal of the American Academy of Religion, Method & Theory in the Study of Religion, Critical Research on Religion, Anthropology Today*, and *Journal of Religion and Film*. She co-hosts a podcast called 時差 "in-betweenness" (@shichapodcast).

Rita Lester, PhD, is Professor of Religion and Director of Gender Studies at Nebraska Wesleyan University in Lincoln, Nebraska. Her research and teaching interests are in religion as discourse, religion in US law, and the construction of religious identities.

Craig Martin, PhD, is Professor of Religious Studies at St. Thomas Aquinas College, Sparkill, New York. His research interests include method and theory in the study of religion, discourse analysis and ideology critique, and poststructuralism. His books include *A Critical Introduction to the Study of Religion* (2017) and *Discourse and Ideology: A Critique of the Study of Culture* (2022). He edits a book series with Bloomsbury titled *Critiquing Religion: Discourse, Culture, Power*.

Martha Smith Roberts, PhD, is Assistant Professor of Religious Studies at Fullerton College, Fullerton, California. Her teaching covers all aspects of religion in culture and the diversity of religious traditions around the world. Her research and writing focus on North American religious diversity and pluralism, race and ethnicity, new religious movements, and religious studies pedagogy. She has written articles on hula hooping, communities of practice, antiracist pedagogy, and religious diversity and pluralism in the United States.

David G. Robertson, PhD, is Lecturer in Religious Studies at The Open University, Milton Keynes, England. His research interests include contemporary Gnosticism, new religious movements, and conspiracy theories in, as, or about religion. His books include *Gnosticism and the History of Religions* (2021) and *UFOs, Conspiracy Theories, and the New Age: Millennial Conspiracism* (2016).

Donovan Schaefer, PhD, is an assistant professor in the Department of Religious Studies at the University of Pennsylvania, Philadelphia, Pennsylvania. He works on the relationships between affect, power, religion, and materiality, with a special interest in how these connect to science and secularism. He is the author of *Religious Affects: Animality, Evolution, and Power* (2015) and *Wild Experiment: Feeling Science and Secularism after Darwin* (2022).

Brad Stoddard, PhD, is Associate Professor in the History and Art History Department at McDaniel College, Westminster, MD. He researches religion in the United States. He is the author of *Spiritual Entrepreneurs: Florida's Faith-Based Prisons and the American Carceral State* (2021) and has edited or coedited several books. He is currently researching the topic of entheogens.

Index

www.ingramcontent.com/pod-product-compliance
Lightning Source LLC
Chambersburg PA
CBHW050717280326
41926CB00088B/3075